—— *A History of* ——
MAINE
RAILROADS

$\mathcal{A}$ History of
MAINE
RAILROADS

MAJOR BILL KENNY, USAF (RET.)

Foreword by Former Maine Governor John Baldacci

THE
History
PRESS

Published by The History Press
Charleston, SC
www.historypress.com

Front cover, bottom: Boston and Maine steam engine #2 (2nd) 0-4-0, Class F3, circa 1890. *Courtesy Robert E. Chaffin Collection, Boston and Maine Railroad Historical Society Archives.*

First published 2020

Manufactured in the United States

ISBN 9781467145299

Library of Congress Control Number: 2019956055

For my granddaughter, Madelyn Sophia, and the fond memories I have watching her enjoyment, huge smile and sparkling eyes as she rode on Thomas the Train, a full-size "two-footer" steam locomotive. May her future journeys on trains and through life bring her as much enjoyment.
With love, Papa

CONTENTS

CONTENTS

FOREWORD

I have known Bill Kenny for many years, since childhood, when my father owned the Baltimore Restaurant in Bangor at the same time Bill's father owned the Riviera Restaurant in Old Town. This background helped both of us develop the strong work ethics Mainers are noted for. Ironically, both restaurants were located near rail lines, which contributed to our interest and fascination with railroads. Our membership in the Woodford's Club, a social club in Portland, has given us many opportunities to have numerous discussions concerning Maine and its railroads. We both have had a lifelong love of railroads and continue to study how the Maine economy and its railroads are intertwined. We have also frequently commented on the fact that former Maine governor and Civil War general Joshua L. Chamberlain pushed legislation through the state legislature in 1867 to allow the issuance of public bonds to finance the state's railroads for the first time in Maine's history. This contributed greatly to the establishment of Maine's railroads. *A History of Maine Railroads* is a great contribution to the railroad world. I am very pleased to be writing this foreword endorsing a fine book chronicling Maine's railroads, and I believe it will definitely add to your reading enjoyment.

One of my favorite memories is when the Bangor and Aroostook Railroad used to add additional passenger cars to its trains to transport the high school basketball team fans all the way from Aroostook and Penobscot Counties to the city of Bangor for the state basketball tournament each March and add additional late departures to transport them home after the games, with some leaving Bangor after midnight.

Throughout my political career, first as a U.S. congressman from Maine, where I served on the Transportation Committee for ports, airlines and railroads and the Subcommittee on Railroads from 1995 to 2003, and then as Maine's seventy-third governor from 2003 to 2011, I have been working on sustaining, maintaining and expanding railroads in the United States, especially in Maine. Working with Maine's senior senator Olympia Snow, who served on the U.S. Senate Finance Committee, we were able to find the necessary funding to tackle the challenges Maine's railroads and businesses were facing in the late 1900s and early 2000s. Maine senators Susan Collins and Angus King are continuing this work today.

How we move people and freight has always been a challenge as we look for more efficient and effective ways. Our roads are becoming crowded and are breaking down from all the heavy truck traffic. But trucks take what we need and want door to door, and trains don't. Policymakers in Maine have struggled with trying to solve this dilemma for years. Circumstances have changed throughout history and continue to change today. What worked in the 1800s didn't work as well in the mid-1900s. What worked in the mid-1900s doesn't work well today. So it's critically important to study what worked in the past and what might work better going forward to get people and freight to their destinations in a timely and cost-effective manner.

Bill Kenny has extensive experience in railroads, from managing two short-line U.S. Air Force railroads, one in Alaska and one in Maine; to moving hundreds of tons of equipment from the United States and Europe to Saudi Arabia to prepare for and support Desert Shield/Desert Storm in the first Gulf War; to moving oversize and outsize equipment around the world for the paper industry following his twenty-two-year career as an air force officer. These experiences, coupled with his study of past and present railroads in Maine, make Bill the perfect author to write this book. This book is about railroads but also about how railroad policy and economics intertwine and why it has been so important throughout Maine's history. He explains how railroads connected businesses and farmers with deep-water ports in Eastport, Searsport and Portland and how important it was and still is to connect with Canadian cities and Canadian railroads and to the ports of Montreal, Quebec and St. John for shipping around the world.

Bill Kenny examines where and why railroads were built; who was involved in getting them built; and the foresight, courage and ambition needed to establish these rail lines. You will also learn which communities throughout the state were established and/or expanded as a result of railroads. Did you know that more than ninety communities in Maine had electric trains (trolleys) powered by overhead electric wires? One was as short as two miles long, others traveled dozens of miles to connect with other towns and cities and one even traveled between the United States and Canada.

This fascinating and significant contribution to railroad history in Maine will surely find a welcome place on your bookshelf and provide you with a very interesting, little-known chapter of Maine's story. Backed by impeccable research and extraordinary material, Bill Kenny has given us a book to enjoy that reminds us that Maine's history can be found in the most unexpected places. This very informative new take on a part of the history of Maine will bring reading pleasure to everyone, including railroad buffs and historians and those who simply love reading about past events and happenings in their Maine towns.

—John E. Baldacci
Seventy-Third Governor of Maine

Acknowledgements

I n my quest for information, technical data, photographs and documents, I have received assistance from many individuals, organizations, libraries and especially historical societies. It would be impossible to recognize all these individuals and organizations, but I greatly appreciate their support. Any omission of acknowledgement to any person contributing material is unintentional. A few individuals, organizations and historical societies went above and beyond in helping me in my research. I extend special thanks to them:

Stan Jordan, a longtime friend and golfing partner, who worked for the Maine Central Railroad for twenty-three years, culminating as assistant chief engineer, for his advice and guidance and especially for lending me more than five decades of the *Maine Central Messenger*, the monthly magazine provided to active and retired employees, customers and friends of the Maine Central Railroad.

John E. Baldacci, seventy-third governor of Maine and lifelong friend, for writing the foreword and editing the manuscript.

Dr. Timothy Kenny, my son and advisor, for reformatting photos and editing portions of the manuscript.

David Buczkowski, president of the Wiscasset, Waterville and Farmington Railway Museum in Alna, Maine, for providing me photos and permissions and reviewing the narrow-gauge chapter of the manuscript.

Laurie Nanni, president of the Oakfield Historical Museum, for providing photos and permissions.

ACKNOWLEDGEMENTS

John Feero, president of the Belfast and Moosehead Lake Railroad Museum in Belfast and Unity, Maine, for providing photos and permissions.

Carolyn Small, curator of the Cumberland Historical Society, for providing stories from the past, photos and permissions.

James Shea, president of Friends of Bedford Depot Park, for providing photos and permissions.

Al Churchill, St. Croix Historical Society, for providing photos and permissions.

Natalie Liberace and Ben Stickney, Maine State Museum, for doing a lot of research and providing photos.

Patrick Layne, Bangor Public Library, for doing a lot of research and providing photos.

Rick Nowell, archives chairman of the Boston & Maine Railroad Historical Society, for providing a photo.

Sofia Yalouris, Maine Historical Society, for doing a lot of research and providing photos.

And KK for proofreading, because every writer needs the support of a good librarian!

INTRODUCTION

Most of the nineteenth- and twentieth-century railroads in Maine are gone now. At one time, in the early to mid-twentieth century, passenger rail service flourished, as did freight service. Maine has an illustrious railroad history. It was one of the first states to build railroads and trolleys, partly due to the shipping of goods to deep-water ports along Maine's coast and the state's proximity to Canada.

Shipping goods was particularly challenging in Maine because of its vast geographical area and the sparse, spread-out population. Small industries, like sawmills, were starting up all over the state, and they needed a way to ship their goods in a timely manner. Railroads were the answer. The first railroads were short and financed by the owners of the sawmills and other small businesses who started building these railroads across the state. Some were only a few miles long, and others stretched from the Maine/New Hampshire border to points in northern Maine and to Quebec and New Brunswick, Canada. Several of these first railroads were narrow-gauge (two-footers) that were cheaper to build, maintain and operate and were built for specific local purposes.

Building and operating railroads is not an easy task. The logistics of "getting the right stuff to the right place at the right time for the right price" has always been a challenge in Maine. It has also been difficult to find investors to back railroad expansion in the state unless and until it made economic sense and was profitable. These investors knew that railroads were expensive and took years to build, along with the expense of maintaining and operating the rail lines, but Maine's need to accommodate supply and demand provided the perfect situation for them.

As Maine businesses grew, so did the need for railroads. Two of Maine's governors were very instrumental in ensuring that Maine railroads were built and/or saved from abandonment: one governor in the mid-1800s and one in the late 1900s/early 2000s. The governors, the investors and the many businesses all contributed to the success and history of Maine railroads.

From the mid-1800s to the 1950s, there was a huge demand for rail freight and passenger travel in Maine. The passenger travel was met by trolleys in addition to trains. At one time, more than ninety Maine communities offered trolley service. Through all these years, rail service has met the demands and challenges of carrying passengers and shipping products from one part of the state to another and, over the years, has adapted. There is still a strong presence of railroading in Maine today, evidenced by the many railroad lines serving Maine, including the popular Downeaster Amtrak, Pan Am Railways, the St. Lawrence and Atlantic Railroad and the Central Maine and Quebec Railway.

I have had a lifelong interest in trains. When I was eleven years old, I took my first train trip. My father pinned my name and the names and telephone number of my grandparents on my shirt and put me on a passenger train in Old Town, Maine, to travel by myself, under the watchful eyes of the conductor, 125 miles to Portland, Maine, where my grandparents were waiting for me at Union Station. On this trip, the conductor took me around with him after leaving each station as he punched passenger tickets and greeted everyone. This was the beginning of my passion for railroads. As an adult, another highlight was a thirteen-hour train journey from Fairbanks to Anchorage, Alaska. It was a marvelous experience. The Alaska Railroad train traveled through the "bush," where the train would stop for those living in this wilderness area of Alaska where there were no roads or electricity. People would put red flags on the trees to let the engineer know they needed a ride to the next town for supplies. I actually got to eat Alaskan salmon cooked on a wood stove in a 1960s dining car; what a treat that was. This, of course, enhanced my enthusiasm for railroads. Later, in my U.S. Air Force career as a logistics war planner and joint special operations officer, I was again involved with trains. I oversaw the air force short lines that brought munitions and shipments of coal for the heating plants to Loring Air Force Base in northern Maine and to Eielson Air Force Base, just south of Fairbanks, Alaska. We had our own air force locomotives at both bases. During the buildup for Desert Shield/Desert Storm in the early 1990s, it was my job to "get the right stuff to the right place at the right time for the right price." I had to plan huge shipments by ship, truck and railroad. We had to get battle tanks for the army shipped from where they were being built in Ohio and Michigan to ports on the Atlantic coast to load on ships to take to Saudi Arabia, all shipped by rail. It was also my job to move heavy equipment across Europe, particularly Germany, by rail to put on ships at Hamburg, Germany, to ship to the Gulf region.

Today, I still enjoy traveling on the various railroads and visiting the many train and trolley museums across the United States, meeting the dedicated railroad workers and volunteers at the railroad and trolley museums and those who operate the historic railroads. I am particularly fascinated with studying the railroad routes and how they came about.

This book chronicles the history of Maine railroads and the railroads' contributions to the growth of the economy of the state of Maine. As Maine railroads were established, so were towns and cities. It also reflects the work ethics of Maine's citizens and entrepreneurs by telling the story of how and why these many railroads were built. To understand the progressive history of Maine, study the remarkable establishment of its railroads and the people involved. It will give you a deep appreciation and understanding of how important railroads were to the world in the past and still are for our world today. This book will introduce you to the interesting and varied world of Maine railroads and take you on a trip through Maine's past. All of the railroads in Maine's history couldn't be included in this book, but my goal is to provide you a sampling of the railroads and trolleys to stimulate your further interest in finding out even more about the history of Maine railroads.

Welcome aboard and enjoy the ride!

Chapter 1

KEY PLAYERS

JOHN ELIAS BALDACCI, SEVENTY-THIRD GOVERNOR OF MAINE

John Elias Baldacci, who served as the seventy-third governor of Maine from 2003 to 2011, was born on January 30, 1955. He also served as a member of the United States House of Representatives from 1995 to 2003.

In the House of Representatives, Baldacci served on the Transportation Committee and the Subcommittee on Railroads, where he focused on keeping the country's railroads—especially those in Maine and other New England states—operating fully and effectively and increasing passenger service by rail. He was a huge advocate for Amtrak and, specifically, bringing more Amtrak passenger travel to Maine.

As governor, Baldacci initiated many reforms on a wide range of issues including healthcare, energy development and public education. He also focused on keeping the railroads in Maine operational. He felt keeping railroads fully operated and updated was not only important to the railroads but also to the farmers and other businesses in Maine, especially in Aroostook County, the northernmost county in Maine. This was a difficult challenge, as railroads weren't very profitable and were allowing the infrastructure, especially the railbeds and tracks, to deteriorate to the point that the Montreal, Maine and Atlantic Railway, the railroad serving northern Maine, petitioned to abandon tracks that were no longer profitable. It was here that Governor Baldacci took great initiatives to save this vital rail link to northern Maine. He proposed and got voter approval for the state to issue bonds for the state to buy this trackage, and he appealed successfully to President Barack Obama to get a $10.5 million grant to repair and maintain the railroad. He also focused on purchasing the International Marine Terminal in Portland and the port terminals at Searsport and Eastport. The updating of the International Marine Terminal was instrumental in his successor luring a major international container shipping company to expand operations in Portland. This had an enormous positive economic effect on the railroads as well, as containers shipped via rail throughout the state.

Finally, Baldacci's vision to have Amtrak service expanded to Maine came to fruition beginning with service in 2001 in Maine.

Benjamin Edward Bates IV, Rail Industrialist and Textile Tycoon

Benjamin Edward Bates IV was born on July 12, 1808, in Mansfield, Massachusetts. He attended various private schools and enrolled at Wrentham Academy, where he studied from 1823 to 1825. John G. Davis met Benjamin Bates in the early 1830s, and the two later became business partners. They met while Bates was a clerk for Barnabas T. Loring at the B.T. Loring Company on Washington Street in Boston. Taking what he learned about the dry good business, Bates partnered with Davis and another partner, John N. Turner, to start the Davis, Bates & Turner craft goods and services company in the early 1830s. After the closing of that firm, he served for a short while as president of the Union Pacific Railroad from August 1, 1849, to May 3, 1850, at which point Alexander DeWitt, an acquaintance and textile mill owner in Oxford, Massachusetts, talked with him about opportunities in Lewiston, Maine. This convinced Bates to move to Lewiston and enter the mill business, opening the Bates Mill in 1852. He quickly expanded to build the Bates Manufacturing Company in Lewiston. He was a very successful businessman and the richest person in Maine from 1850 to 1878. The Bates Manufacturing Company was the largest employer in Lewiston and one of the largest in the state of Maine. He also founded the Lewiston Power Company to build a dam to provide power to the mills and to create a canal system in Lewiston.

Bates had great foresight. He anticipated that the talk of secession by the southern states prior to the Civil War indicated that there would be a shortage of cotton. He purchased an enormous amount of cotton prior to the Battle of Fort Sumter—so much that he cornered the cotton market. The shortage of cotton resulted in Bates having a monopoly, which drove prices skyrocketing and caused dozens of New England businesses to go out of business.

Bates's canal system and mills were modeled after the textile mills in Lowell, Massachusetts. While Biddeford, Saco, Augusta, Waterville and Brunswick also had textile mills, the Bates Mill in Lewiston was by far the largest. The Bates Mill began the transformation of Lewiston from a small farming community into a textile manufacturing center.

Bates needed more workers than he could find to work in his mills in the early 1860s, so he sent "recruiters" to find workers in nearby Quebec, which had high unemployment and poverty levels. These Canadien workers were enticed by the job opportunities since they could travel by train in less than one day from Montreal to arrive at the Grand Trunk Station in Lewiston to find temporary work in the mills and return home by train. But many of the Canadiens stayed permanently in Lewiston, settling in an area within walking distance from the mills that became known as "Little Canada." Lewiston has remained Franco-American since this migration. By 1890, the population of Lewiston had risen to over 21,000, up from 1,800 in 1840. So many Canadiens migrated through Lewiston that it became known as the "Ellis Island of Maine."

Getting the needed workers for his mills was only one way for Bates to use railroads effectively. He was president and on the board of several railroad companies in Maine. In addition to having served as president of the Union Pacific Railroad, the largest railroad presence in Maine at the time, he used his wealth to help finance the construction of railroads throughout Maine. He benefited by receiving materials and shipping finished cotton and other textile products via rail. Bates also coordinated the movement of war materials for use in the Civil War by railroads throughout Maine.

Bates was a very religious person and a huge contributor to the Maine State Seminary in Lewiston. His contributions were so significant that it was renamed Bates College.

Benjamin Bates died on January 14, 1878, at age sixty-nine, in Boston, Massachusetts.

Joshua Chamberlain, Civil War General and Thirty-Second Governor of Maine

Joshua Chamberlain was the first of two Maine governors who were instrumental in the growth and survival of railroads in Maine. He was one of three Civil War Union generals to serve as governor of Maine. He was born in Brewer in 1828. He attended the Bangor Theological Seminary for three years but dropped out and accepted a teaching position at Bowdoin College in Brunswick. It was at Bowdoin that he met Harriet Beecher Stowe and Frances "Fanny" Adams, the latter a daughter of a minister and Chamberlain's future wife.

When the Civil War broke out in April 1861, Chamberlain resigned from Bowdoin and enlisted and accepted a commission from Maine governor Israel Washburn as a lieutenant colonel in the Twentieth Maine Infantry Regiment. On July 2, 1863, the second day of the Battle of Gettysburg, Chamberlain fought back the Fifteenth Alabama at Little Round Top, which was on the far flank of the Union forces. Holding that line was essential to prevent the advancing Confederate army from breaching the line and getting behind the Union army. He had 386 men in his regiment, including two of his brothers. The fighting was intense, and the Twentieth Maine suffered 120 casualties. His regiment was running low on ammunition and couldn't hold the defensive for much longer, so he made a risky but heroic decision: he ordered the attack downhill toward the larger opposing force. The move was successful, with the Twentieth Maine capturing more than 300 Confederate soldiers of the Fifteenth Alabama. Chamberlain protected the flank, all while suffering two wounds himself. General Ulysses Grant later stated that the battle at Little Round Top saved the Union army from being surrounded by Confederate troops. Chamberlain was promoted to brigadier general following the Battle of Gettysburg. President Abraham Lincoln later brevetted (promoted) him to major general. Chamberlain was later awarded the Medal of Honor for his bravery.

A little-known fact about Chamberlain relates to a significant battle at the Union army railroad junction in Harrisburg, Pennsylvania. This was a major railroad junction where more than half of all the supplies from the North were shipped South toward the fighting. Chamberlain warded off the attack by the advancing Confederate army led by General Robert E. Lee, thus keeping the critical supply lines open.

Major General Joshua Chamberlain was also selected by General Ulysses S. Grant to review the parade of the Confederate infantry as part of the formal surrender at Appomattox in April 1865. As the Confederate infantry marched by, Chamberlain ordered the Union army standing in review to salute the passing Confederate soldiers. The Confederate general leading the passing army ordered his troops to return the salute. It is tradition for a surrendering army to lay down its weapons. But Major General Chamberlain ordered that the Confederate soldiers could keep and return home with their weapons.

Following the Civil War, Chamberlain went back to teaching at Bowdoin College, now as a full professor. But he wanted to serve in other ways, so in 1866, he ran for and was elected governor of Maine. At that time, governors stood for election every year, unlike in present days. He was elected by 62 percent of the vote in 1866, a record-winning percentage at the time, and in 1867 he won by 72 percent of the vote, setting another record, one that hasn't been equaled in Maine history. He served for four consecutive terms as Maine's governor. During his tenure in office, he was instrumental in persuading President Lincoln to grant Maine a "Land Grant College." That college is now the University of Maine.

But Chamberlain also made history in Maine railroading. Prior to 1867, railroads in Maine could not issue public bonds to fund the building of railroads. Governor Chamberlain was successful in getting legislation passed, and he signed a bill into law allowing investors in railroads to use public bond funding. This was significant in the building and expanding of railroads in Maine. You can read more about this in chapter 2 under the section "Bangor & Piscataquis Railroad & Canal Company."

In 1871, Chamberlain left the governorship and became president of Bowdoin. He was in ill health as a result of the wounds he received fighting in the Civil War and, as a result, retired from Bowdoin in 1873. Chamberlain spent the remaining years of his life writing and speaking about the war. He wrote his memoir of the Appomattox Campaign, *The Passing of the Armies*, but it was not published until after his death. He died on February 14, 1914.

John R. Graham,
Innovative Business and Railway Entrepreneur

John R. Graham was born of Scotch-Irish parents in Enniskillen, County of Fermanagh, Ireland, on December 19, 1847. He moved to Boston with his parents a year after his birth. Times were tough for the Graham family, as his father had extreme difficulties supporting a growing family. So, at ten years old, Graham not only attended school but also worked for one dollar a week and board. He left school at thirteen to enter business life. He served with the Union army in the Fourth Massachusetts in the Civil War. Graham's older brother suggested he take up shoe manufacturing, so for thirty years that is what he did; he organized and managed a shoe factory in Quincy, Massachusetts. Graham Shoe was extremely successful and known up and down the Atlantic Seaboard. Using the profits from his shoe company, Graham started looking at acquiring and developing real estate. He bought many dilapidated buildings, rehabilitated them and sold them at a profit.

In the early 1890s, Graham took on the challenge to use his business skills to reorganize the Quincy and Boston Street Railway Company, which was in receivership at the time. Few thought the railway company could be saved, but Graham did it and did it quickly Within a few short months, the railway company was once again profitable. He oversaw the merging of the Quincy and Boston Street Railway with the larger Bay State Company. At the same time, Graham served as general manager of the Brockton Street Railway system from 1898 to 1902. He was often sought out for advice and recommendations for railways across New England.

In May 1902, Charles A. Coffin, co-founder and president of the General Electric Company, contacted Graham because of his abilities to turn failing businesses around and asked him to travel to Bangor, Maine, to investigate the general condition of the Public Works Company in Bangor, for which General Electric had a major financial interest. This company was not profitable, and General Electric wanted to know what could be done to turn the company around to make it profitable again like Graham had done with the Quincy and Boston Street Railway and the Brockton Street Railway. This is the trip that brought Graham to Maine.

John R. Graham was impressed with the Bangor of 1902. He saw the potential for Bangor, being at the head of Maine's largest river, the Penobscot, to become the gateway to central and northern Maine, particularly to be the shipping port for the vast agricultural and lumber riches of Maine. He also saw the prospect of making Bangor a resort area for tourists. Graham was so impressed with Bangor's possibilities that he submitted a favorable report to the General Electric Company. He accepted the position of general manager and treasurer for the Public Works Company and served in that position from 1902 to 1905. He led the way to raise enough capital to purchase the entire holdings of the company, and he formed the Bangor Railway and Electric Company, the immediate predecessor of the Bangor Hydro-Electric Company. This new company consolidated all the properties of the street railway, electric lighting and water departments of the old company and remained profitable from that point on. Utilizing the assets and profits from this company, Graham started building his trolley lines throughout the Bangor region.

Graham was one of the promoters of the Lewiston, Augusta and Waterville Railway and was also instrumental in the success of the Portland Street Railway and Cumberland County Power and Light Company. He served as director on many public utilities, banks and industrial manufacturing companies throughout Maine. Graham had a love for horse racing, owning Constantine, a renowned racehorse of his day. He was also fond of quoting Shakespeare. He led a full and active life traveling the world in his later years. John R. Graham died in Intervale, New Hampshire, on August 24, 1915.

W.S. Libbey:
"Finest Electric Railroad in All New England"

W.S. Libbey was born in Avon, Maine. Avon borders Phillips and Strong near Farmington in Franklin County. As a young boy, Libbey moved with his family to West Waterville. He farmed his land, studied medicine and taught school. He studied law for a short while in Waterville and taught himself telegraphy, the skill to operate a telegraph, by watching the telegraph operator at the train depot. He was enamored of this new means of communication, and within a year, he was hired to be a telegrapher in Auburn by the Western Union Telegraph Company. He served Western Union in its Newburyport, Massachusetts office and in West Waterville, Maine, as well. But Libbey wanted to pursue business interests rather than continue as a telegraph operator. And he felt Lewiston gave him the best opportunities.

In Lewiston, Libbey began a small business supplying sawmills and bobbin manufacturers with timber. Taking the advice of his father-in-law, he learned all he could about textile manufacturing and bought a small cotton mill in North Auburn. Taking the profits he earned from that small mill, he restored a run-down woolen mill in Vassalboro, making it a successful operation within two years of his purchase. He did all this while continuing his work as a telegrapher for the Western Union. He traveled by train to Vassalboro after work on Saturday to run the mill in Vassalboro all day on Sunday and then took the two-hour trip back on Sunday evening to be at work in the telegraph office first thing Monday morning.

Libbey then took over the managing of a mill in East Dover that was losing money by getting financing from the Deering-Milliken textile firm in

New York. Deering-Milliken was always looking for new sources of woven goods to sell, and it was the perfect source for Libbey to get financing. In return, Libbey gave Deering-Milliken the best products the mill produced. He also became friendly with Harry Dingley, the son of Congressman Nelson Dingley. The Dingley family was worth millions from their publishing business, a catalogue business that eventually become the publisher of the L.L. Bean and other advertising catalogues. Harry worked in the same building in Lewiston where the Western Union office was located. This building was where the *Journal* was published, and they depended on the telegraph for all news outside the Lewiston-Auburn area. The *Journal* is still an active newspaper, called the *Lewiston-Sun Journal* today.

In 1888, Libbey was successful enough that he could leave his job as a telegraph operator at Western Union, and with money borrowed from the Dingley family, he purchased the Cumberland Woolen Mill in Lewiston. Business was so good that he bought the idle Lincoln Mills that had been built beside the Androscoggin Falls in 1845 to manufacture cotton goods. The mill was renamed the W.S. Libbey Company at that time. He updated this mill with all new machinery, making his mill one of the most productive in the New England states.

Libbey then purchased the American Light and Power Company and the Lewiston and Auburn Electric Light Company. This was a significant move. Now that his electric companies were producing all this power, they needed customers. This is what led Libbey to think of building an electric railroad to use this cheap power. So he set forth to build not just an electric railroad in Lewiston and Auburn but what became known as the "Finest Electric Railroad in All New England." He built the Portland-Lewiston Interurban (PLI) electric railroad, connecting Portland, Maine's largest city, to the south to Auburn and Lewiston. It took four years to build this railroad, and it began daily trips to and from Portland in 1914. The PLI operated from 1914 to 1933, the longest-running electric railroad in New England.

George Mansfield

George Mansfield, a local businessman in Hazelhurst, Massachusetts, became enthralled after seeing the Ffestiniog Railway when visiting the country of Wales. This railroad used two-foot spacing (actual width 23½ inches) between the rails. He saw this as a more economical way to build railroads than using the standard 56½ inches between the rails. He promoted this idea to residents of Bedford and Billerica, Massachusetts. Billerica, while not enthusiastic about getting a railroad, saw the success the Middlesex Central Railroad was bringing to Bedford. The townspeople of Bedford and Billerica realized the benefits of having a railroad connect to the Middlesex Central Railroad, where it could further connect to the Southern Division of the Boston and Lowell Railroad and points beyond; they simply couldn't find an investor to make it happen, nor could they raise the money themselves. George Mansfield proposed the building of a two-foot railroad from Bedford to Billerica and showed how this could be built economically. He also showed the people of Billerica how little upfront money would be needed, easing their concerns. He showed Bedford how it would benefit as well by explaining how this would help connect through Billerica to the Boston and Lowell Railroad going north. Construction began in May 1877, and the line from Bedford to Billerica, a distance of 8.63 miles, was completed. It was built very cheaply, as promised. The new Billerica and Bedford Railroad also built turntables at each end, an engine house in Bedford and a wye, which is a triangle of railroad track used for turning locomotives or trains. No other stations were built along the line. The railroad went bankrupt just a year later in June 1878 and liquidated its locomotives and rolling stock. The Boston and Lowell Railroad saw the demise of the Billerica and Bedford Railroad line as a way to increase its passenger ridership, so it replaced the two-foot rails with standard-gauge rails and continued to use this line for both freight and passenger service until 1962, when the line was abandoned due to more passengers traveling by car and more freight going by truck.

With the demise of the Billerica and Bedford Railroad, George Mansfield looked north to where residents and businessmen in Franklin County, Maine, were looking for an economical way to build a railroad. Building a standard-gauge railroad in this part of Maine was not economical because of the rough terrain. But Mansfield traveled to Maine to show them how the narrower two-foot gauge railroad could be the answer. He ended up organizing the Sandy River and Rangeley Lakes (SR&RL) Railroad, buying the locomotives and rolling stock from the bankrupt Billerica and Bedford Railroad and setting up its headquarters in Farmington, Maine. It was in Farmington that the new railroad could intersect with the standard rail width Maine Central Railroad to connect with nearby Strong, Phillips and Rangeley. Mansfield became the manager for this new railroad. You can read more about the Sandy River and Rangeley Lakes Railroad, the Franklin and Megantic Railway and the Kingfield and Dead River Railroad in chapter 3.

John Poor

John Alfred Poor, a Bangor lawyer, was concerned about Maine's economic decline in the 1840s and had an idea about how to reverse it. Poor, a native of Andover, Maine, had gone to school in Bangor, taught school briefly and then studied law with an uncle in Bangor. He and the uncle went into practice until the latter retired. Poor and his younger brother then opened a law practice together, also located in Portland. Portland had fallen on tough times; the clipper ships were gone, and grass was growing through the cobbles of India, Pearl and Exchanges Streets.

Poor learned the geography and commerce of northern New England during his travels as a young man. He developed an early appreciation of the potential of railroads and was first inspired when he viewed a steam locomotive on the Boston and Worcester Railroad in 1834. Poor conceived railroads radiating from Portland to Montreal to the west and Halifax to the east. Poor decided that Portland should make a bid to be the winter port for Montreal. Montreal had built numerous canals to get agricultural products from the countryside to the city where they could be shipped out but had a problem in winter when the St. Lawrence River iced over. The Montreal Board of Trade looked for an alternative and was talking with a delegation from Boston, which wanted to become the port Montreal used in the winter months. John Poor wanted Portland to be the terminus for an international railroad connecting the United States with Canada and for Portland to be the primary American port in the Northeast. The two cities were in fierce competition. The delegation from Portland, led by Poor, was carrying copies of Boston's newspapers reporting how Boston Harbor was iced over at the time the two delegations were visiting Montreal and did so most years for a few days, whereas Portland's harbor had only iced over for two days in the past thirty years. Those representing Portland felt this gave them an advantage in presenting why they should be selected over Boston.

Poor arrived in Montreal in February 1845 to convince the board of trade that Portland was the best choice for a winter port. His account of his trip through high snowdrifts and frigid temperatures suggests his determination and that of his backers in Portland and elsewhere. With Poor and the Boston delegation both in Montreal, several of Poor's associates were traveling by sleigh to catch up with him. They wanted him to have important information that they felt could sway the vote toward Portland as their choice of a warm-water winter port. They brought with them the latest European news that had arrived in Boston and some mail destined for Montreal. Their goal was for Poor to show that mail shipped from Portland rather than the usual route from Boston could get to Montreal faster. They were successful in this feat, as they traveled with this news and mail to Montreal in thirty-one hours. The "usual Boston route" through Concord, New Hampshire, and Burlington, Vermont, had taken more than sixty-two hours previously. Judge William Pitt Preble, a prominent judge and businessman from Portland, was traveling with the Poor delegation. He carried a very important piece of paper to give to Poor: the charter from the Maine legislature with its official seal granting the St. Lawrence and Atlantic Railroad Company the right to build a railroad. This was significant because Portland was ready to build the railroad right away and Boston was not; Boston did not yet have a charter for a railroad from the Commonwealth of Massachusetts. Poor walked into the board of trade meeting in Montreal at 10:00 a.m. on May 10 dramatically holding up this charter granted by the Maine legislature on February 10. After hearing the information about how mail and products could travel faster from Portland to Montreal than from Boston and seeing Portland was ready to start constructing the railroad right away, the Montreal Board of Trade selected Portland and then proceeded to organize its own part of the railroad.

Construction on the railroad began on July 4, 1845, with a public ceremony in Portland. Poor almost singlehandedly was responsible for the 1845 charter of the St. Lawrence and Atlantic Railroad Company. The railroad connecting Portland and Montreal through western Maine wilderness and New Hampshire's mountains was completed in 1853.

In 1846, Poor started a foundry on Fore Street in Portland to build railroad locomotives and cars for the St. Lawrence and Atlantic Railroad. The Portland Company built many hundreds of steam locomotives, engines, construction equipment, automobiles and other products until it closed in 1978, when it could no longer compete.

John Poor died on September 6, 1871, but his legacy lives on today with the railroad lines he helped create still operating in Maine today.

William Vance

William Vance was born in Londonderry, New Hampshire, in late 1759. In 1775, he marched as a sixteen-year-old fifer in the Revolutionary War on the side of the thirteen colonies against the British until his discharge in 1780. In May 1785, he switched his allegiance to the British and moved to St. David, New Brunswick, Canada, with Loyalist group Cape Ann Association when he received a land grant on St. David's Ridge near St. Stephen, New Brunswick, from the British government. He practiced law in St. Andrews, was a justice of the peace in New Brunswick and was otherwise a loyal British subject. Most of his business interests were now in Maine, however, so he moved to Baring. He later leased and subsequently bought the land from Lord Baring that was then called "Vance's Mill" and is now the town of Baring.

Shortly after his arrival in Baring, Vance was elected to be a member of the Constitutional Convention of 1819, which voted to separate Maine from Massachusetts. In 1820, the year Maine became a separate state, he was named land agent on the St. Croix River and appointed to construct a road from Baring north to Houlton. He was elected to the Maine state legislature, representing Plantation 6 in 1823, and elected in 1825 and 1827 representing the town of Calais. He represented Baring in the Maine legislature in 1828 to 1829.

Vance had five wives: Nancy Stewart, Jane Parker, Mary Bell, Charlotte Holland and Charity Stafford. He had little formal education but made his way building lumber mills along the St. Croix River, the river between Maine and New Brunswick, Canada. His first mills were built in what is now called Vanceboro. The challenge he faced was how to get the lumber from his mills in Vanceboro sixty miles southeast to the port of Calais. The town of Vanceboro is named for him. Vanceboro became significant in Maine railroad history when it became a very large railroad terminal for the European and North American Railway that went from Bangor to Vanceboro in the 1860s. Subsequently, the St. Croix–Vanceboro Railroad bridge was built so the trains could connect with Canadian railroads.

Vance built new lumber mills in Baring and across the river in Milltown, New Brunswick. These mills were still six miles up the river from the port of Calais, and while that was better than sixty miles away like they were near Vanceboro, he still faced the challenge to get his lumber to the port to put on ships for export around the world. So he started the Calais Railroad, later changed to the Calais and Baring Railroad. This is alleged to be the first railroad built in Maine and the second in the United States. The charter from the State of Maine for the Calais Railroad was granted in 1832. Construction began three years later, and it became very profitable over the years as lumber could more easily and economically be transported from the mills upriver to the port of Calais, one of the deepest ports on the East Coast. The railroad still exists as a branch of the Maine Central Railroad (MEC) connecting to its Bar Harbor branch.

In addition to the town of Vanceboro being named after William Vance, the town of Charlotte, Maine, was named for his daughter. Vance died in 1842 in Readfield, Maine.

General Samuel Veazie, Railroad and Business Tycoon

General Samuel Veazie was a prominent businessman in Bangor, Maine. He was born on April 22, 1787, in Portland. A tireless entrepreneur, Veazie built ships, sawmills, a dam, a bank and other businesses. He also purchased a railroad.

He moved to Topsham, ten miles north of Portland, for a while, where he owned a merchant ship. Shortly after his arrival, he purchased the Androscoggin Boom, a system of guiding and sorting logs floated down the river to lumber mills.

After serving as a general in the War of 1812, Veazie began purchasing lumber mills in Bangor and Old Town and built a dam to power these mills. In 1834, he established the Veazie Bank in Bangor. In 1854, he purchased the Bangor & Piscataquis Railroad & Canal Company, which later was renamed the Veazie Railroad Company. This railroad later became part of the Maine Central Railroad. Freight still travels over those tracks today.

Veazie, the largest property owner in Bangor at the time, thought Bangor's property taxes were too high, so in 1853, he led the effort for a portion of Bangor to secede from Bangor and become a separate town. That town is named after Veazie. He owned almost all the property in town.

During his lifetime, Samuel Veazie owned four stores, a hotel, a dam, several sawmills and even the Congregational church.

General Veazie died in Veazie on March 12, 1868.

Joseph Whitney

Joseph Whitney was an entrepreneur who erected sawmills to take advantage of the annual river lumber drives down the Machias River to what became the town of Whitneyville. He built a dam across the Machias River to power the mills. Whitney, along with John Palmer and Cornelius Sullivan, built a narrow-gauge railroad to carry the sawed lumber from Whitney's sawmills down the Machias River to the port of Machiasport, where it could be loaded onto ships and shipped worldwide. This railroad was the second built in Washington County and the third in the state. The *Phoenix*, the first steam locomotive used on this line, was shipped from Boston. The second, the *Lion*, arrived three years later. You can see the *Lion*, one of the earliest surviving steam locomotives in America, in the Maine State Museum in Augusta.

Chapter 2

WHY DID MAINE NEED RAILROADS?

aine has been noted for several things over the past two centuries: timber products, potatoes, textiles, paper products, fishing and blueberries. Maine should be remembered, as well, for its railroads. While seldom mentioned in published histories of Maine, railroads played significant roles in moving its people, agriculture, timber and other resources.

Maine doesn't have any Class I railroads today, although Amtrak serves parts of the state. Many regionals and short lines remain. Elected leaders in Maine government believe that some remaining lines need to be saved, so in 2010, the state purchased a major section of the former Bangor and Aroostook Railroad property to save it from abandonment.

Maine was in a unique position to contribute to the feeding and housing of the country at the time Maine became a state in 1820. Maine had, and still has, some of the deepest harbors in the world, and most of the products produced in the United States were shipped by sea. Maine is a huge state—more than 350 miles from the New Hampshire border to Madawaska at the top of the state bordering Canada. Maine was basically an agrarian society at that time. There were a great deal of other resources in the state, including more than seventeen million acres of forest land and mineral resources, such as granite, lime, slate and ice. All of these were in great demand in other parts of America and the world. While lumber and other products were in great demand, how do you get these products to the ports, especially during winter months when the rivers were frozen over? How do you get products from all over Maine overland to the southern states where they were in great demand? Well, one answer is through building railroads. While money from wealthy investors was available to connect the major population centers in Maine, building smaller railroads to connect the less populated areas of the state wasn't economically feasible. They simply couldn't make enough profit to do this. At that time, it wasn't legal to use public funds, like the issuance of bonds, in Maine to finance railroads. That law wasn't changed until 1867 following the Civil War.

Railroads played a significant role in the development of Maine during the Industrial Revolution, which began in the early 1800s. Maine was also home to the nation's premier shipbuilders during that period. It was difficult for these shipbuilders to get the lumber and masts they needed from the forests during the winter months. Most of the logs deep in Maine forests were cut and moved by sled-driven horses over the frozen ground to the nearest river so they could be transported in log drives downstream to the mills.

Log drive. *Maine Historical Society Item #100595, Collections of Westport Island Historical Society.*

Massive log jam at Pishon's Ferry, Skowhegan, 1870. *Maine Historical Society Item #8990, Collections of Skowhegan History House.*

If the ice in the rivers was slow melting or melted too fast, log jams would happen, slowing down delivery of the logs to the mills. This caused enormous financial problems not only for the loggers but for the financiers and mill owners as well. Moreover, log driving was a very dangerous job. Many serious injuries and deaths resulted each year from accidents along Maine rivers. These log drives congested the entire river for weeks at a time. When logs were being driven downriver, the river was not passable for boat traffic, so that became a problem as well.

Was there a more efficient and cost-effective way to get lumber to the customers in southern Maine and around the country and world? Railroads became part of the answer. If you had rail connections to the main railroads in the major cities in Maine, sawmills could be built closer to where the trees were felled. The lumber could then be transported by rail to major rail lines and to the ports along the Maine coast for shipment around the world.

A few lumber barons controlled what mills were built and where. Samuel Veazie, Ira Wadleigh, Abner Coburn and Rufus Dwinel bought entire townships, constructed sawmills and competed against one another for control of the dense forests. They also competed to redirect water to serve their needs. Lumbering created boomtowns, such as Bangor, which for a time was the world's greatest lumber shipping port. Bangor was perfectly situated on the Penobscot River and connected to a major railroad. Lumber shipped out of Bangor on ships and rail. The first sawmill in Bangor was built in 1772, and by the mid-1800s, Bangor had more than three hundred sawmills, earning it the title "Lumber Capital of the World."

Sawmills were built throughout Maine in the early 1800s, but it was small entrepreneurs who started building smaller railroads to get the logs to the sawmills and lumber from the sawmills to the ports and to connect to major railroads coming from New Hampshire north through central Maine to service the major population centers.

It All Began Downeast with Short-Line Railroads: Calais Railway

The building of the short-line smaller railroads, sometimes shorter than two miles long, by entrepreneurs began in downeast Maine. The origin of the phrase "downeast" is typically traced to nautical terminology referring to direction rather than location. In the warmer months most suitable for sailing, the prevailing winds along the coast of New England and Canada blow from the southwest, meaning ships sail "downwind" to go east. The northeastern areas are said to be "downeast" in relation to major cities such as Boston. Therefore, sailors spoke of going "up to Boston" from downeast ports, such as Portland, Searsport, Eastport and Calais, Maine, even though Boston is about fifty miles south of Maine.

One of the first railroads built in Maine was the Calais Railway, which was granted a charter by the State of Maine in 1832. Construction began three years later. The name was changed to the Calais Railroad in 1838, and it became a two-mile railway from Calais to Salmon Falls in 1839. This line was extended about six miles up the St. Croix River to transport lumber from the sawmills owned by William Vance to the tidewater in Calais, where the lumber could be loaded onto ships. The mills spanned the St. Croix River from Baring on the American side to Upper Mills on the Canadian side. At first, there were no train locomotives; horses pulled the cars over the tracks right up until 1841, when the line was abandoned. The railway was reactivated eleven years later and renamed the Calais and Baring Railroad when the tracks were extended to Baring. Lewy's Island Railroad came along in 1854, connecting the Calais and Baring Railroad from Baring through Princeton and on to Forest City, Maine, and Forest City, New Brunswick, Canada. (These Forest City communities have the unusual distinction of sharing the same name.)

The Calais and Baring Railroad reported having hauled 34,623,217 feet of long lumber, 41,232,000 laths, 753,300 pickets, 444,500 shingles, 600 ships' knees and 6,000 cords of mill-wood end edgings. So much lumber was moved between the mills that the port of Calais was second only to Bangor as the busiest lumber port in Maine at that time.

In 1870, the railway was reorganized as the Saint Croix and Penobscot Railroad (StC&P). The rail line continued to expand when, in 1893, the Washington County Railroad received its charter from the state, connecting it to the Maine Central Railroad's (MEC) Bar Harbor branch at Washington Junction, near Ellsworth. The Washington County Railroad was completed in 1898, becoming the Calais branch in 1911 after MEC gained controlling stock interest in 1904.

Bangor & Piscataquis Railroad & Canal Company

The state's second railroad traveled from Bangor to Old Town along the west bank of the Penobscot River for eleven miles. The Maine state legislature granted a charter on February 18, 1833, to the Old Town Railway Company owned by Samule Smith and Rufus Dwinel. Work began that year on the line. The roadbed was upgraded partway from Bangor to Orono, and some bridge piers were constructed across the rivers and streams on that section. Then, the work stopped due to lack of funding. Smith and Dwinel sold their charter and the right of way to the Bangor & Piscataquis Railroad & Canal Company for $50,000, and construction began again on November 29, 1835. The first train ran from Bangor to Old Town on November 29, 1837.

The owners spent $500,000, or about $40,000 per mile, for the completion of the roadbed, stations, engines, cars and bridges.

This train had an average speed of around six miles per hour, and the rail gauge was four feet, eight inches, with the earliest rails being strap iron spiked to six-inch planks, fourteen inches long. This unstable construction wasn't very good; the rail would often come loose from the plank and go right up through the floors of the coaches. In 1849, these tracks were upgraded to "chair rail" and, in 1867, upgraded further to the more stable "T" rails. The railroad inventory consisted of six locomotives, the first of which was the *Pioneer*; two carriages for passengers; a baggage car; and several freight cars. The locomotives were built by the Robert Stephensen Company at Newcastle-on-Tyne, England. They were drop hook engines that had no control over their speed; they moved either forward or backward at full power, which was about twelve miles per hour. The engines did not have cabs. This meant that the engineer and fireman were exposed to all sorts of weather—snow and cold in the winter and heat in the summer sun—as they stood on an open platform on the back of the engine loading wood and operating the train.

It was not part of the engineer's job to watch the track ahead for signals and obstructions as it is on trains today. This job was done by a man who rode on top of the first car behind the engine. If this lookout saw anything that required stopping the train, he notified the engineer by pulling a cord that connected to a bell next to the engineer.

The passenger cars were basically stagecoaches equipped with flanged wheels. The conductor walked alongside on a footboard corresponding to a footboard of an open trolley collecting tickets through the windows of the cars/coaches. The coaches were heated in the winter months in a very unique way. A couple of hours before the train was ready to depart, two ten-gallon cans of heated water were placed in each passenger coach to preheat it. Just before the train departed, those two cans were replaced with two other ten-gallon cans of hot water. This provided the heat necessary for the twelve-mile journey. The average train that ran at one time consisted of one engine, one or two passenger cars, a baggage car and two or three freight cars. They transported laths, shingles, clapboards, lumber and, of course, passengers. The train ran three times daily, and the price of a one-way ticket was thirty-seven cents.

Upon the arrival of the train at the terminals in Bangor and Old Town, the locomotive was detached and placed in a roundhouse for servicing. Yard workers and the freight handlers who normally loaded and unloaded

The *Pioneer* locomotive. *Courtesy of Bangor Public Library.*

cargo from the trains worked to realign the cars in the order needed for the trip back the other way.

The Bangor and Piscataquis Railroad would connect to the Bangor and Katahdin Railroad in 1891 to form one of Maine's longest-running railroads, the Bangor and Aroostook Railroad (BAR). For the first time, iron ore from Katahdin Iron Works, near what is now the town of Milo, and agricultural products like potatoes could be shipped from northern Maine.

The Bangor & Piscataquis Railroad & Canal Company had a thirteen-year run until the company ran into legal trouble when tracks for the railroad crossed land owned by General Samuel Veazie. General Veazie sued the railroad, and as a result of this litigation, he ended up owning it. General Veazie renamed it the Bangor, Old Town and Milford Railroad Company (BO&M) after he built a bridge in 1849 across the Penobscot River from Old Town to Milford. General Veazie was a lumber baron who owned eighty sawmills and various real estate holdings in Bangor, and this railroad was constructed primarily to haul timber products from his and his competitors' sawmills to Bangor. Owning the railroad was a perfect fit for his business plans; he controlled not only most of the sawmills in the area but now also owned the way to transport the lumber. He ran the company until his death on March 12, 1868, after which his heirs continued operating the railroad until the European and North American Railway purchased it in 1869.

The original intent for this railroad was to connect Quebec to the ocean ports in Maine by joining with another railroad. This was very ambitious but unsuccessful. The initial attempt began with a charter granted by the Maine legislature on March 9, 1836, for the Belfast and Quebec Railroad. The Province of Quebec had to pass similar legislation for this to happen. A glitch occurred because the railroad didn't have enough private investment for this to happen, and at the time, Maine didn't allow public funding through the sale of bonds. The financial panic in 1837 further exacerbated the attempt, as private investment was hard to come by. There was another attempt in 1845 that also failed. A contributing factor for these failures was that many citizens in Belfast, Maine, were interested in a canal, which was part of the original plan, but weren't interested in the railroad portion. The Maine statutes were subsequently changed to allow public funding for the building of railroads in 1867 following the end of the Civil War. The law was signed by Civil War general Joshua Chamberlain, who was by then Maine's governor.

The Civil War helped the nation realize how important railroads could be to our nation's economy as the armies of the Union and the Confederacy moved a huge amount of cargo, supplies and troops through the states. Joshua Chamberlain was instrumental in spiking the interest of Maine citizens and, of course, potential investors. During the Civil War, it was General Chamberlain who helped save the Union junction at Harrisburg, Pennsylvania, from being captured by General Robert E. Lee's Confederate army. The train junction at Harrisburg was one of the main railroad interchanges in the North; more than 65 percent of all the trains carrying supplies from the North southward connected here. So had General Lee succeeded, critical supplies for the Union army would not have made it to where the fighting was happening in the South. Historians point out that had General Chamberlain not successfully warded off General Lee at Harrisburg, the entire outcome of the war could have been different.

The European and North American Railway (E&NA), formerly the Bangor and Piscataquis Railroad, began operating in October 1871. Its intent was to link New York with Canada and, via ships, to Europe. This would be the final step in the transcontinental railroad linking Halifax to San Francisco and Europe. President Ulysses S. Grant, under whom Maine governor Joshua Chamberlain served in the Union army during the Civil War, was part of the delegation that dedicated the line at Bangor in October 1871. Other members of the delegation were the governor general of Canada, Lord Lisgar; Speaker of the House Hannibal Hamlin; cabinet secretaries; and the mayor of Bangor, among others. There was a parade, military review, fire engine trials, a regatta and a reception for the president's party held at Bangor.

President Grant rode the train from Bangor to Old Town, making stops along the way to meet the enormous crowds waiting to see him. Schoolchildren serenaded him and presented him with bouquets on Broadway Street in Bangor. Maine regiments who served in the Civil War passed in review of President Grant, and it is reported that several Civil War veterans broke through the barriers to shake hands with their former commanding general.

The European and North American Railway operated from its completion in 1871 until it was leased to the Maine Central Railroad in 1882. In 1889, the International Railway of Maine was built by the Canadian Pacific Railway (CPR) from Megantic, Quebec, to the MEC at Mattawamkeag, Maine. The MEC granted trackage rights to the CPR over the 56-mile section from Mattawamkeag to Vanceboro at that time. In November 1955, MEC purchased the entire 114-mile E&NA for $3,115,500. On December 17, 1974, the CPR purchased the 56-mile Mattawamkeag to Vanceboro section from MEC for $5.4 million. MEC maintained ownership of the 58-mile Bangor to Mattawamkeag section. In 1981, MEC was purchased by Guilford Rail System, now Pam Am Railways, which continues to operate the Bangor to Mattawamkeag section. CPR applied to abandon the Mattawamkeag-Vanceboro section effective January 1, 1995; however, it was taken over by the Eastern Maine Railway, which continues to operate the line.

Some confuse the Bangor & Piscataquis Railroad & Canal Company with another railroad with a similar name, but the Bangor and Piscataquis Railroad is a different railroad. The Bangor and Piscataquis Railroad extended from Bangor to the Milo-Brownville area to carry freight from Brownville and iron ore from Ore Mountain, near Milo, smelted at the Katahdin Iron Works. The Bangor and Piscataquis Railroad, along with the Katahdin Iron Works Railroad, combined to form the Bangor and Aroostook Railroad in 1891. The Bangor & Piscataquis Railroad & Canal Company eventually became part of the Maine Central Railroad, as mentioned earlier.

PORTLAND, SACO AND PORTSMOUTH RAILROAD

The third railroad in Maine was the Portland, Saco and Portsmouth Railroad (PS&P). It was incorporated on March 14, 1837. This was a significant development in the expansion of railroads in Maine because for the first time, the railroad connected Portland to Boston, as it connected to the Eastern Railroad in Kittery via a bridge to Portsmouth, New Hampshire. This railroad opened on November 21, 1842 and was fifty-one miles in length.

In 1872, the PS&P was bought by the Eastern Railroad, and in 1884, the Boston and Maine took over the Eastern Railroad, including the PS&P, operating it as the Boston and Maine Eastern Division. In the 2000s, portions of the PS&P were converted to a biking and walking trail known as the Eastern Trail. The Eastern Trail, as it exists in 2019, is a very popular sixty-five-mile biking and walking trail that starts at the Piscataqua River in Kittery, Maine, just across from Portsmouth, New Hampshire, and ends in South Portland.

Palmer and Machiasport Railroad (Later Renamed Whitneyville and Machiasport Railroad)

The Palmer and Machiasport Railroad was completed in 1843 to transport lumber from the Eastern Mill and Land Company sawmills in Middle Falls, later called Whitneyville, to load onto ships in Machiasport. The Eastern Mill and Land Company was owned by Joseph Whitney of Calais and a group of lumbermen and landowners. The mills at Whitneyville included ten single saws, six lath machines, a shingle machine and a clapboard machine. Over one million shingles per year were shipped over the Machiasport Railroad. Eight round trips were made daily over the railroad pulled by two locomotives, the *Lion* and the *Tiger*. These locomotives would alternate; one day the *Lion* would pull the train to the port and return, and the next day the *Tiger* would do the same. On the alternate days, each locomotive would move cars around the yard at Whitneyville.

Twenty-three years later, in 1866, James D. Pope bought controlling interest in the Eastern Mill and Land Company and changed its name to the Whitneyville Agency. He renamed the railroad the Whitneyville and Machiasport Railroad at that time.

One of the railroad's locomotives, the *Lion*, has historical significance. The *Lion* was built by Hinkley & Drury Locomotive Works in 1846. It is the oldest known American-built locomotive in New England. It was listed in

The *Lion* locomotive. *Item #86.3.1, Collections of Maine State Museum.*

the National Register of Historic Places in 1976. The *Lion* is prominently displayed as the first exhibit when entering the Maine State Museum in Augusta. The locomotive is twelve and a half feet long by seven feet tall by four and a half feet wide and is made of solid oak timbers with iron strapping. It has a five-section boiler with a dry stream dome at its center, from which steam flows to the steam chest driving the pistons that move the train. The boilers and cylinders are insulated with a thin layer of wood covered by a thin layer of iron. The main stack is located in the front and has an unusual inverted cone shape, most likely intended to deflect sparks and cinders that came from the exhaust.

The Whitneyville and Machiasport Railroad ceased service in 1892.

Androscoggin and Kennebec Railroad

The Androscoggin and Kennebec (A&K) Railroad received a charter on March 28, 1847, and by January 1850 had built a line between Waterville and Danville (now Auburn). It connected with the Penobscot and Kennebec (P&K) Railroad at Waterville and with the St. Lawrence and Atlantic Railroad, which came online in 1853. The line ran from Danville, near Lewiston, to Waterville and was built in three sections for a total of fifty-five miles, the final section completed in July 1849. This line intersected with the St. Lawrence and Atlantic, running from Portland to Montreal, at Danville. For the first time, there was now a direct route from Bangor west to Danville, where it connected with the St. Lawrence and Atlantic and on northwest to Quebec, Canada, and south to Portland and points south. Both the Androscoggin and Kennebec Railroad and the Penobscot and Kennebec Railroad later became part of the Grand Trunk Railway.

Bridgton and Saco River Railroad

The narrow-gauge Bridgton and Saco River (B&SR) Railroad operated in the Bridgton and Harrison area, connecting with the Portland and Ogdensburg Railroad, later known as the Maine Central Railroad Mountain Division, from Portland to St. Johnsbury, Vermont, near Hiram, Maine, on the Saco River.

The interchange yard at Bridgton Junction with the Portland and Ogdensburg was unique because the Portland and Ogdensburg was standard gauge and the B&SR was a narrow two-foot gauge. The B&SR had six northbound spurs plus a turntable with a single-stall engine house. The freight house was dual gauge for loading and unloading narrow-gauge equipment on standard-gauge cars. There was no runaround track, so southbound B&SR locomotives uncoupled their train on the main line, moved into the yard through a turnout and let their train roll past them into the yard by gravity to avoid being trapped at the end of the spur.

The B&SR design was based on the two-foot gauge Forney engine design originally designed for the Sandy River and Rangeley Lakes Railroad by Hinkley Locomotive Works. This locomotive design became the standard of the two-footers going forward and was also used by the Monson Railroad and the Franklin and Megantic Railway (F&M). Construction of the

Bridgton and Harrison Railway train headed by Engine No. 8 in front of Bridgton Freight House and Station. *Item #83.84.255, Collections of Maine State Museum.*

Bridgton and Saco River Railroad began in 1882, and trains were operating to Bridgton one year later.

Maine Central Railroad operated the trains from Harrison to Bridgton Junction with four round trips daily. There were two separate trains operating to meet the daily trips, which started at 5:15 a.m., with the last run at 8:45 p.m. between those two towns. The first train consisted of a baggage car, a railway post office (RPO) car and a couple of passenger coaches. The second train was the same with an additional feature of a few bench seats at the end of the RPO car to accommodate smokers. The trains also carried freight. The most common freight carried were outbound lumber, pulpwood, apples and canned corn, manufactured goods, grain and feed. Inbound freight consisted mainly of coal and petroleum products. The locomotive, designated #8, was the last locomotive built for the Maine two-foot gauge railways.

Locomotive #8 is historically significant because it derailed in 1930 at a time when the railway was barely profitable. This locomotive was the heaviest locomotive on any two-foot gauge railway, and the derailment was caused due to the thirty-five-pound rails sagging under the weight. This was the beginning of the end for the B&SR. It did become a tourist train for a while, but when iron was needed for World War II, much of the rails were scrapped. The rolling stock, however, was moved to Massachusetts to operate for another fifty years on the Edaville Railroad. After the later restructuring of the Edaville Railroad, the historic Bridgton and Saco River Railway equipment returned to Maine. Some of the rolling stock is now located at the Maine Narrow Gauge Railroad Co. and Museum located on Fore Street in Portland.

The Penobscot and Kennebec Railroad

The building of the Penobscot and Kennebec Railroad (P&K) was instrumental in expanding rail service to connect Bangor and Waterville. At Waterville, the P&K connected with the Androscoggin and Kennebec Railroad (A&K), and at Northern Maine Junction, near Hermon just south of Bangor, it connected with the Bangor and Piscataquis Railroad. In 1845, the year the P&K was chartered, a law was enacted permitting both the P&K and A&K to consolidate under a new name. The legislation was not acceptable to both companies; thus, the A&K was chartered in 1847. The P&K and A&K did not merge until after the contentious section of the previous merger legislation was repealed on September 9, 1862. The following month, on October 28, 1862, the A&K and P&K merged to form the Maine Central Railroad.

The Belfast and Moosehead Lake Railroad

The Belfast and Moosehead Lake Railroad (B&MLRR) was a standard-gauge short-line railroad that began operations in 1871 over a single track from Belfast to Burnham Junction. Grain for poultry, fish oil, leather, coal, lumber and fertilizer shipped southbound and northbound freight consisting of processed fish, shoes and other manufactured goods from Belfast and farm products from Waldo, Brooks, Knox and Thorndike and milk from Turner. For its first fifty-five years, it was operated under a lease agreement by the MEC and known as its Belfast Branch.

It provided passenger and freight stations to eight depots throughout Waldo County. In 1925, MEC canceled its lease, and the B&MLRR ran operations under its own name. Passenger operations ceased in March 1960, although in 1988, the railroad began operating summer tourist trains to offset a decline in freight traffic. In 1991, the City of Belfast sold its interest in the money-losing railroad to private owners. In 2007, the railroad ended

Belfast and Moosehead Lake Railroad locomotive #51, a seventy-ton GE diesel electric locomotive purchased in 1946. *Author photo*.

Belfast and Moosehead Lake Railroad coach undergoing restoration by the Brooks Preservation Society. *Author photo*.

Thorndike Station, built to serve the town of Thorndike on the Belfast Branch of the Maine Central Railroad. This branch later became the Belfast and Moosehead Lake Railroad. This station has been relocated to the Boothbay Railway Village. *Author photo*.

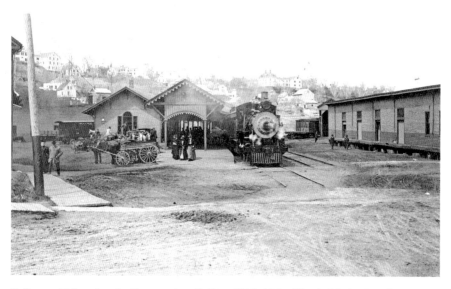

Belfast and Moosehead railway station, Belfast, 1908. *Maine Historical Society Item #98640, Collections of Belfast Historical Society.*

operations as the B&MLRR. Today, the line is operated by the nonprofit Brooks Preservation Society as the Belfast and Moosehead Lake Railway with weekly excursions, except for the winter months, between City Point in Belfast, Waldo and Brooks.

MAINE'S RAILROADS TODAY CONSIST of only regional and short lines. Short lines are what make industries get their goods delivered to major ports and the larger main railroads throughout Maine and neighboring Canada.

Pan Am Railways runs most of the trains in Maine in 2019. It assumed operations of the Guilford Rail System, which owned the Boston and Maine; the Maine Central Railroad; the St. Lawrence and Atlantic Railway; and the Central Maine and Quebec Railway. The St. Lawrence and Atlantic Railway operates the former Grand Trunk, and the Central Maine and Quebec Railway operates the former Bangor and Aroostook Railroad. Other short lines include the Eastern Maine Railway and Turners Island LLC. Turners Island short-line railway connects with Pan Am Railways for shipping destinations nationwide. This is a privately owned and operated fourteen-acre marine-rail cargo terminal located in South Portland that can handle almost any cargo that can be shipped by either rail or sea.

The Eastern Maine Railway Company is an interesting one to look at because it has entered into cooperation agreements with other railroads to connect cities and towns in Maine with those in New Brunswick, Canada.

The Eastern Maine Railway is a 99.5-mile short line owned by New Brunswick Southern Railway Company (NBSR), a holding company that is part of the J.D. Irving industrial conglomerate. The New Brunswick Southern Railway was a historic railway operating in western New Brunswick, Canada, with its headquarters, while an operational railway, in Woodstock, New Brunswick. It was acquired by the Canadian Pacific Railway in 1890, and its operations and name were subsumed by the CPR. The NBSR was maintained by CPR as a non-operating holding company for its land and property in New Brunswick. This company was sold to industrialist K.C. Irving in 1941. All land ownership, including timber holdings and railway rights of way, transferred to the Irving conglomerate, while CPR retained ownership of the physical railway assets and the right to operate them.

The original NBSR lines were built to 3 feet, 6 inches (1,067 millimeters) narrow gauge. These tracks were converted to 4 feet, 8½ inches (1,435 millimeters) in 1881. The change in gauge made it more connectible to major railroad lines. Together with its sister company, the New Brunswick Southern Railway, the NBSR lines form a continuous 189.5-mile main line connecting St. John, New Brunswick, Canada, with Brownville Junction, Maine. Another sister company, the Maine Northern Railway, operates a separate 258-mile railway system connecting Millinocket with Van Buren.

The Eastern Maine Railway Company also operates a short line for Woodland Rail. Woodland Rail is a freight-only 11.83-mile located in both Maine and New Brunswick. It exists to connect the pulp mill in the part of the Washington County town of Woodland referred to as Baileyville with the Milltown Spur, owned by the New Brunswick Southern Railway, at the midpoint of the Salmon Falls Railroad Bridge, which crosses the St. Croix River and the Canada-U.S. border between Calais, Maine, and St. Stephen, New Brunswick. This crossing point between the two countries is significant because there are customs operations there for both. This part of Woodland Rail is the "middle section." From its interchange with New Brunswick Southern Railway at the Salmon Falls Railroad Bridge in Calais, the line runs southwest for approximately 2.5 miles to St. Croix Junction.

From St. Croix Junction, the line continues southwest up to the St. Croix River valley as the Woodland Spur 1.7 miles to Baring, Maine, the line that crosses from the southwest of the St. Croix River to the northeast bank at Upper Mills, New Brunswick, on the Baring Railroad Bridge.

The line then continues northwest for 5.08 miles in New Brunswick to Mohannes, New Brunswick, where it crosses back to the southwest bank of the St. Croix River at Woodland Junction on the Sprague Falls Railroad Bridge. At Woodland Junction, an industrial spur runs south for 1.0 mile to serve the Woodland Pulp thermo-mechanical pulp mill in Baileyville. The Woodland Spur continues northwest for 1.0 mile to end at the oriented strand board mill.

Another 12.6-mile section of the former Calais Branch between St. Croix Junction and Ayers Junction remains in place but is not in service. The Maine Department of Transportation purchased this section to preserve the rail infrastructure should service be restored to the port of Eastport.

There are about one thousand miles of active railroad in Maine, half of the amount that existed in the 1920s. The only passenger train in Maine in 2019 is Amtrak, and that is limited to one train, the Downeaster. The Downeaster currently stops in Brunswick, Freeport, Portland, Saco, Old Orchard Beach and Wells.

Chapter 3

HISTORY OF THE TWO-FOOTER

SMALL ENGINES, BUT BIG "ECONOMIC" ENGINES FOR MAINE BUSINESS AND INDUSTRY

Standard gauge was favored for railway construction in the United States. Standard-gauge tracks are four feet, eight and a half inches between the rails. Narrow-gauge tracks are two feet between the rails, although a few narrow-gauge railroads have tracks that are three feet, six inches between the rails. Narrow-gauge lines were built in many areas to minimize construction costs for industrial transport or resort access, and some of these lines offered common carrier service. All of the narrow-gauge railroads in Maine were two-footers. Narrow-gauge railroads were built in a few other states, but the spacing between the rails was three feet between the rails.

BIRTH OF THE TWO-FOOTERS

While this book is about Maine railroads, two-foot gauge railroads actually had their beginnings in Billerica and Bedford, Massachusetts. This background is important because much of the rolling stock (train engines and cars) ended up as part of the Bridgton and Saco River Railroad, Monson Railroad and Sandy River and Rangeley Lakes Railroad in Maine. So for historical purposes, let's talk a bit about the Billerica and Bedford Railroad.

The Billerica and Bedford Railroad

Top: Ariel locomotive. *Courtesy bedforddepot.org.*

Bottom: Billerica and Bedford Railroad commutation ticket. *Courtesy bedforddepot.org.*

The Billerica and Bedford Railroad in Massachusetts was America's first two-foot common railway. Key to the introduction of two-footers to Maine was George E. Mansfield of Hyde Park, Massachusetts, who had recently returned from a trip to Wales in 1875. It was in Wales that Mansfield observed the Festiniog Railway. This carrier used track of just two feet, twenty-three and a half inches between the rails. (By contrast, most American railroads by this time had adopted the present standard gauge of four feet, eight and a half inches.) The Festiniog caught the fancy of Mansfield; he went on to build a small test track in his backyard to study the principles of a miniature-gauge railway. This two-footer was a perfect passenger solution for a train to connect with the Boston and Lowell Railroad, which ran between the main Massachusetts cities of Lowell and Boston. When the Billerica and Bedford Railroad company ceased to exist, the engines and cars were sold to Sandy River and Rangeley Lakes Railway, which Mansfield helped establish.

Sandy River and Rangeley Lakes Railroad: America's Longest Two-Foot Railroad

George E. Mansfield, general manager of the Billerica and Bedford Railroad in Massachusetts, traveled to Maine to meet with citizens and business leaders in Franklin County who were looking for a way to travel and get manufactured products to the Maine Central Railroad, which terminated in Farmington. Mansfield convinced the people that a two-footer was the most economical way to get this done. Two-footers required less grading, smaller ties and rails and smaller locomotives and rolling stock than wider, standard-gauge railroads. The resort area in northern Franklin County wanted passenger transportation to the towns of Rangeley, Strong, Phillips, Kingfield and other stops along the way. There was also no way to ship manufactured wood products from northern Franklin County, an area of large forests of timber, to Farmington and on to markets to the south. Mansfield thought engines and cars brought to Maine from the now defunct Billerica and Bedford Railroad in Massachusetts and the less expensive rail beds and rails could be the answer for northern Franklin County.

The Sandy River and Rangeley Lakes Railroad was the culmination of several smaller railroads. The first section built was an eighteen-mile railroad, the Sandy River Railroad, which linked the Maine Central Railroad hub in Farmington with Phillips via Strong in 1879. In 1883, the Franklin and Megantic Railway linked up in Strong to continue to Kingfield, and soon after, the Kingfield and Dead River Railroad connected Kingfield all the way through Carrabassett and Bigelow.

The Franklin and Megantic Railway

Construction for the Franklin and Megantic Railway, formerly the Franklin and Megantic Railroad, began in 1884. This 14.6-mile railroad started at the Sandy River in Strong and was built primarily to access the forests on the slopes of Mount Abram in Salem Township. This line served several sawmills from Strong to Kingfield. In 1899, the line was extended to a large sawmill in Crockertown, later called Bigelow, near the Canadian town of Megantic (Lac-Mégantic, Quebec). This Crockertown is the one in Franklin County, not to be confused with a town of the same name in Penobscot County.

Building this line was challenging because the mountain in Crockertown (Bigelow) is the second highest in Maine, with Mount Katahdin being the highest. So there were steep slopes to climb and valleys and gorges to bridge.

This line was built using twenty-five-pound rail, which didn't serve well. This was replaced with thirty-five-pound rail about ten years later. Shortly before Salem, the Mount Abram Branch, also known as the Mountain Branch, a short two-mile railroad, was built to help the land barons farther up toward Mount Bigelow get their forests harvested and the logs to sawmills. The main purpose was to supply logs to sawmills that sprouted up along the way to the Franklin and Megantic so the sawed lumber could get to the Maine Central Railroad in Farmington and to markets to the south. This line only lasted until all the usable logs were taken. The branch line was

Combination Car #1, Franklin and Megantic Railroad. Placed in service on August 7, 1885. Later acquired by the Sandy River and Rangeley Lakes Railroad in 1908. One of the few coaches left in its original state. It is now on display at Boothbay Railway Village. *Author photo*.

removed in the early 1900s. This railroad was one of the most scenic two-footers in Maine, but snow plagued it throughout the long winter months. From the first winter, 1884–85, the Lilliput trains were continually getting lost in snow drifts and having to be shoveled out by hand.

KINGFIELD AND DEAD RIVER RAILROAD

Josiah L. Maxey, a Gardiner banker who had recently financed construction of the Kennebec Central Railroad, purchased controlling interest of the Sandy River Railroad in 1892 and then the majority stock in the Franklin and Megantic Railway in 1897. Under Maxey's direction, F&M purchased the Kingfield and Dead River (K&DR) Railroad at auction on August 2, 1898. The F&M, K&DR and Sandy River railroads operated under common management until they formally merged as the SR&RL in January 1908.

The Kingfield and Dead River Railroad was opened in 1894 and ran from Kingfield to Carrabassett, a distance of nine miles. Its main reason for existence was to open the new forest areas owned by the barons who were also shareholders of the railroads. The K&DR was only a "paper company." The F&M owned it, and the F&M ran it. It had no engines or rolling stock.

Carrabassett was only an agency station, which it shared with the U.S. Post Office. In 1900, an additional six miles of track was added from Carrabassett to take the trains into the agency station of Bigelow.

Wiscasset, Waterville and Farmington Railway

The Wiscasset, Waterville and Farmington (WW&F) Railway was the second two-foot gauge railway system that served Maine during the late 1800s and early 1900s, after the Sandy River and Rangeley Lakes Railroad. The Wiscasset and Quebec (W&Q) Railroad was the predecessor of the WW&F, the last two-footer system started, opening in 1895 between Wiscasset and Albion.

The original goal of the W&Q was to open a rail route between the deep-water port of Wiscasset and Quebec, Canada. This goal was abandoned, however, when the Maine Central Railroad wouldn't give W&Q permission to cross its rail line in Burnham.

During the first decade of the 1900s, the W&Q reorganized as the Wiscasset, Waterville and Farmington Railway, and its expansion plans turned northwestward toward Farmington and a connection with the Sandy River and Rangeley Lakes Railroad two-foot system. The WW&F rails

Wiscasset, Waterville and Farmington Railway train approaching Head Tide station. *Item #83.84.251, Collections of Maine State Museum.*

Wiscasset, Waterville and Farmington Railway locomotive #9 at WW&F Railway Museum in Alna. *Author photo.*

reached only as far as Winslow, failing to cross the Kennebec River into Waterville en route to Farmington. The resulting fifty-eight-mile system, extending from Wiscasset to Albion and Winslow, would be the WW&F at its greatest length.

A new trolley line would emerge in the second decade of the 1900s, creating competition for passenger and freight traffic for the WW&F from the Winslow Branch. By 1915, the competition was too much, and the branch was abandoned.

The remaining WW&F would survive until the early 1930s. On June 15, 1933, the morning train down from Albion jumped the tracks just north of the Whitefield iron bridge. That morning, the train was heading to Wiscasset carrying, among other passengers, sixty-five Freemasons from Waterville on their way to visit the Freemasons' chapter in Wiscasset. The derailment occurred while the train was climbing an incline where it passed over a short bridge when Engine #4 jumped the tracks down into a shallow brook. The boxcar, express car and postal and baggage cars piled up, but the two passenger cars did not derail, and no one was injured. This wreck became known as the "Masons' Wreck." Each year, the Freemasons take a ride on the WW&F Railway from the WW&F Railway Museum in Alna to enjoy a picnic near where the wreck occurred.

"Masons' Wreck" on Wiscasset, Waterville and Farmington Railway in Alna, September 12, 1905. *Item #90.30.6, Collections of Maine State Museum.*

Rather than rerail the train and continue operations, WW&F owners chose to shut down the impoverished railroad.

The WW&F Railway Museum is a great place to visit. There is a railroad turntable there, as well as a Model T rail car and the only surviving two-foot locomotive built by the Portland Company that pulls the scenic train.

The Kennebec Central Railroad

The Kennebec Central Railroad is one of the most interesting narrow-gauge railroad stories in Maine history. This five-mile-long railroad was constructed solely to offer transportation for American Civil War veterans and to transport coal and other products between the city of Gardiner and a soldiers' home in the town of Togus, Maine. Another interesting and unique fact about the Kennebec Central Railroad is that it didn't connect with any other railroad at all.

Train service began in July 1890, serving the needs of an estimated 2,800 veterans living at the soldiers' home. There was a passenger terminal on the Randolph side of the river with stairs leading up to the covered bridge across the river to Gardiner on the other side. Coal was unloaded on the Randolph side of the river into a large government-owned coal shed and then onto flat rail cars to a trestle in Togus, where it was unloaded and used for the steam-heating plant for the soldiers' home buildings. Initial rolling stock was six flatcars and two boxcars built by W.H. Dyer of Strong, Maine; two passenger coaches; and a combination passenger-baggage car built by Jackson & Sharpe. The sixteen-ton Forney locomotive was built by Baldwin Locomotive Works.

The railroad settled into a profitable routine of four round trips per day from Randolph to Togus with a couple of coal gondolas between the engine and the combination passenger-baggage car to ensure continuing the transportation of coal that was so critical to heating the many buildings of the soldiers' home. The railroad purchased a used nineteen-ton engine built by the Portland Company from the Bridgton and Saco River Railroad when its first engine wore out in 1922 and purchased another used eighteen-ton Forney engine from the Sandy River and Rangeley Lakes Railroad to replace the second engine in 1926.

As renowned chronicler of Maine two-foot railroads Robert C. Jones demonstrates in *Two Feet to Togus: The Kennebec Central Railroad*, running the trains was hardly dull. "The employees faced such challenges as Maine's harsh winters and, even worse, a regular procession of inebriated veterans on their way back from a little 'R&R' in town." There was even a little municipal competition, as an electric railroad from Augusta soon offered veterans a choice of destinations. In its heyday, the home was a popular destination for local residents in search of entertainment or just a nice place to spend the day. Baseball games, theater, band performances and an animal park attracted overflow crowds almost every weekend. Eventually, the appeal of the home as a destination dimmed, and when the railroad lost its contract to haul coal to Togus, its days were numbered.

Operations were suspended abruptly on June 29, 1929, after the federal government awarded the coal-haul contract to a trucking firm and the railroad was no longer profitable.

Chapter 4

STANDARD-GAUGE TRACKS VERSUS NARROW-GAUGE TRACKS

T rack gauge is measured between the inner faces of the load-bearing rails. Gauge matters because all of the equipment within a network needs to have running gear to match the gauge. The U.S. standard railroad gauge is four feet, eight and a half inches.

Maine developed a unique system of narrow-gauge railroads on track just twenty-four inches apart to lower the cost of railroad construction and operation, allowing them to be built in areas where it wouldn't be otherwise economically feasible. At their peak, the Maine two-footers operated on over two hundred miles of track transporting both passengers and freight in and out of rural Maine. They played a key role in the timber industry as well as early tourism efforts. The companies were the smallest narrow-gauge common carriers in the United States. Other states, like Colorado, used narrow-gauge tracks, but they measured three feet, six inches.

Most of the short-line railroads mentioned in chapter 1 and all of the two-foot railroads in chapter 2 used narrow spacing between the tracks. They were known as "two-footers." The space between the tracks for the two-footers used in Maine was one foot, eleven and five-eighths inches, whereas the standard-gauge railroads used by the major railroads had larger spacing between the tracks.

When building a railroad, cost and ability to meet the desired purpose are generally the two largest concerns. Narrow-gauge railroads tend to cost less to build, but they will have lower load weight limits as well. Standard-gauge railroads cost more at the outset, but weight limits will be higher.

Weight limits affect the hauling ability of the railroad in two ways. The first is that cars carrying more freight will weigh more but will also be able to haul more. The second reason is that higher weight limits generally allow for larger, more powerful locomotives to operate on the line, meaning more freight can be hauled in a single train. In most cases, if you can haul more tons per car and more tons per train, the operating cost per ton goes down.

There are benefits to using narrow-gauge tracks. They are favored in mountainous regions because standard-gauge railroads would be much more expensive to build. Narrow-gauge railroads require less earthwork, smaller bridges, narrower tunnels and a narrower right of way. Because the narrow-gauge train engines and cars are lighter, they are better at climbing steeper grades. As the track gauge widens, the cost of construction, particularly in mountainous areas like western Maine, goes up considerably. The costs and benefits of standard-gauge railroads tend to balance out.

As railroads developed and expanded throughout history, one of the key issues was different railroads using different gauges between the tracks, which meant that loads had to be unloaded from one set of rail cars and reloaded onto others, a time-consuming and expensive process. Because of this, the industry adopted a "standard gauge" of four feet, eight and a half inches, allowing interconnectivity and interoperability.

Narrow-gauge tracks on the Eastern Promenade in Portland. *Author photo.*

Narrow-gauge swing bridge to allow ships to enter Casco Bay. *Author photo.*

Standard-gauge tracks. *Author photo.*

Chapter 5

BOSTON AND MAINE RAILROAD

T he earliest Class I railroad to connect Boston with Portland, Maine, was the Boston and Maine (B&M) Railroad. This railroad was unique because it primarily was a result of the owners acquiring other railroads rather than constructing new lines. There were four distinct divisions of the B&M: the Portland Division, the New Hampshire Division, the Fitchburg Division and the Connecticut River Line. We will only be focusing on the Portland Division for the purpose of this book.

The B&M began with a charter granted by the Commonwealth of Massachusetts in 1833 under the name of the Andover and Wilmington Railroad. Construction began in 1835, and by 1843, the line had been extended to South Berwick (Maine) Junction. A second charter was granted, also in 1835, allowing the extension to Haverhill, Massachusetts, and later that year the New Hampshire legislature granted a charter from the Massachusetts line to the Maine state line under the name of the Boston and Maine Railroad. In 1836, the Maine legislature granted a charter to the B&M extending the line to Portland. The Boston and Maine began transporting passengers in 1845, during the presidency of James K. Polk. It also hauled freight in New England, New York and Pennsylvania. In 1920, the B&M transported forty-three thousand passengers and nearly 23 million tons of freight, earning the company more than $46 million. It had 23,900 freight cars and 1,953 passenger cars in its inventory in 1920, and it now operated in five northeastern states and one Canadian province as well.

Boston and Maine steam locomotive #410. This locomotive has been restored and is on display in Lowell, Massachusetts. *Author photo.*

Shipments of grain, ice, lumber, meat and produce over its rails contributed to the expansion of Boston as a market center and a great seaport. The B&M was instrumental to the growth of New England's manufacturing cities and helped the rural areas of northern New England overcome their isolation from the rest of the country.

It was also the B&M that led the way for tourism in northern New England. As stated on the Boston and Maine Historical Society website, "The delights of Lake Winnipesaukee and the White Mountains, the promotion of seacoast resorts, and the romantic attractions of New England's historic places were captured in B&M view-books, magazines, and extensive newspaper advertising. In the 1930s and 1940s the Boston and Maine Snow Trains were a major boost to the development of the winter sports business."

One of the B&M's most famous passenger trains was the *Flying Yankee*. The B&M faced great challenges, not the least of which was due to a decline in manufacturing in the region and by companies switching to trucks to deliver goods in the twentieth century. To overcome this loss of revenue, the B&M led in the implementation of new technologies to try to stay competitive.

It abandoned unprofitable branches, improved freight handling, upgraded passenger equipment and ventured into the airline and bus businesses.

The *Flying Yankee* covered about 730 total miles a day on its Monday through Saturday trips from Boston to Portland and back, during which it reached speeds of up to 100 miles per hour. After a little over twenty-three years in operation, during which the train traveled over 5.25 million miles, the streamlined *Flying Yankee* made its final trip on May 7, 1957 and was then retired from service. The Boston and Maine ended its passenger service between Boston and Portland in 1965.

During its heyday between the end of World War II and the mid-1950s, the B&M had depots from North Station in Boston stopping at twenty other Massachusetts locations, sixteen New Hampshire stations and fifteen stops in Maine before culminating at Union Station in Portland. The stops in Maine were the Cummings Station in South Berwick; North Berwick Station; two stops in Wells at Wells Beach and the Elms; Kennebunk Station; Arundel Station; Biddeford Station; Saco Station; four stops in Old Orchard Beach at Temple Avenue, Campground Station, Old Orchard Beach Main Terminal and Surfside; and three stops in Scarborough at Grand Beach, Scarboro Beach and Rigby Station.

Union Station, Portland. *Courtesy of Library of Congress LC-DIG-det-4a23196.*

Union Station clock at Congress Square, Portland. *Author photo.*

Union Station was first opened on June 25, 1888, and was the terminus for the Boston and Maine, Maine Central and the Portland and Ogdensburg Railroad lines. It was torn down in 1961. The only remnant of Union Station is its clock. Built in 1888 by the Howard Clock Company in Boston, the Union Station clock has been in its current location since 1982, when it was donated to the City of Portland by the Maine Central Railroad Company. The clock is in a brick-and-glass structure that exposes the original mechanical clockworks to public view. It is operational and was restored in the early 1980s by Walter A. Browne and Parker L. Starrett, who made the clock hands. The clock was once one of the most recognizable features of the Union Station tower at St. John and Congress Streets.

Interstate 95 was completed to Portland in 1956 and extended to Houlton in 1965. That same year, the B&M Railroad discontinued passenger service from Boston to Portland, signaling the triumph of the automobile over mass transportation.

The Boston and Maine Corporation still exists. Although the Boston and Maine name is no longer used, the B&M that began 180 years ago lives on in a form suited to the needs of our time.

Chapter 6

ST. LAWRENCE AND ATLANTIC RAILROAD

The St. Lawrence and Atlantic Railroad (SLR), known as St-Laurent and Atlantique Quebec (SLQ) Railroad in Canada, is a railroad operating between Portland, Maine, on the Atlantic Ocèan and Montreal, Quebec, on the St. Lawrence River. It crosses the Canada-U.S. border at Norton, Vermont, and is presently owned by short-line Genesee and Wyoming Railroad. It came into being because products in Montreal couldn't ship directly to Europe by way of the St. Lawrence River during the winter months when the river was covered with ice and not passable. Shippers in Montreal were looking for a year-round way to ship goods to Europe, and the port of Portland became the answer.

The line was originally built by the St. Lawrence and Atlantic Railroad in the United States and the St. Lawrence and Atlantic Railway in Canada, meeting at Island Pond, Vermont, south of the international boundary. Major communities served included Portland and Lewiston, Maine; Berlin, New Hampshire; Island Pond, Vermont; and Sherbrooke and Montreal, Quebec.

Shipping from Portland, Maine, to Liverpool, England, is one hundred miles closer than shipping from Boston, Massachusetts. Because of this, Portland enjoyed an advantage in the transatlantic trade of shipping timber and agricultural and mining products with the additional savings of more than one day's sailing time. The enormous surge of Canadian products from Montreal to Portland resulted in the building of wharves, piers, stockyards, grain elevators, coal facilities, warehouses and shipyards there, transforming

St. Lawrence and Atlantic Railroad locomotive at Intermodal Terminal in Auburn. *Author photo.*

Portland into one of the busiest and most profitable Atlantic shipping ports on the East Coast of North America.

The St. Lawrence and Atlantic Railroad was chartered by the Maine legislature on February 10, 1845; by the New Hampshire legislature on July 30, 1847; and by the Vermont legislature on October 27, 1848, to build a continuous line from Portland, Maine, northwest into northeastern Vermont. The first section, from Portland to Yarmouth, opened on July 20, 1848. The line was extended to Danville (now Auburn) in October 1848, to Mechanic Falls in February 1849, to Paris in March 1850 and to Bethel in March 1851.

The line was originally built to the Canadian gauge of five feet, six inches (1,676 millimeters) and was converted to standard gauge of four feet, eight and a half inches about 1873. Canadian gauge is also referred to as provincial or Portland gauge.

Shipping by ferry service was a very slow process. Cargo had to be loaded onto the ferry on the Montreal side of the St. Lawrence, unloaded on the other side and then loaded onto the trains destined for the port of Portland. The ferry could carry only about one and a half boxcar loads of cargo and make two or three trips daily. This caused a huge backup waiting to be ferried across the Montreal side of the St. Lawrence River. Due to these significant demands on the ferry service across the St. Lawrence River to and from Montreal, the Victoria Railroad Bridge was built and opened in 1860. When the bridge was completed, the continuous rail cars of one train could carry more cargo across the St. Lawrence directly from Montreal in one day than could be accomplished in thirty days using the ferry. The average number of rail cars traveling across this bridge from Montreal within two years of its completion was seventy-two freight cars and five passenger rail cars per week.

The railroad became enormously successful only when the Grand Trunk took over operations and the railroad tracks were completed all the way from the port of Portland to Montreal.

The St. Lawrence and Quebec Railway still operates today with seventy miles of track in Maine, fifty-eight miles of track in New Hampshire and thirty-four miles of track in Vermont. The railroad interchanges with the New Hampshire Railroad in North Stratford, New Hampshire, and Pan Am Railways in Danville Junction (Auburn), Maine. It carries aggregates, chemicals, food and feed products, intermodal containers and steel and scrap.

Chapter 7

GRAND TRUNK RAILWAY SYSTEM

The Grand Trunk Railway became North America's first international railroad. It came into being in 1853, when a group of English investors led by Sir Francis Hincks purchased the St. Lawrence and Atlantic Railroad. Hincks was determined to have a main trunk line from eastern Canada to ice-free ports on the Atlantic Ocean in the United States. The St. Lawrence and Atlantic Railroad did just that, as it ran from Montreal to the Vermont border and later to the port of Portland. It was one of the most significant contributions to Maine's economy when it was completed. Its headquarters was located in London.

The Reciprocity Treaty in 1854 between Canada and the United States eliminated customs tariffs between the two, and the resulting increase in trade with the United States—which in part replaced trade with the United Kingdom—led to an economic boom in Canada and in New England as well. This railroad was instrumental in creating the first international trade agreement between Canada and the United States. Economic growth was stimulated further when the American Civil War began in 1861. War supplies produced in Canada and Maine could be transported more quickly and consistently by rail. For example, Benjamin Bates, owner of one of the textile mills in Lewiston, Maine, bought and shipped as much cotton by rail as he could find from other textile mills, and the Bates Mill became the main supplier of textiles for the Union army during the four-year war. Even though the textile mills in Saco were larger and produced more textiles, the five Bates Mills in Lewiston became the most prosperous textile mills in the

Portland, Me., Grand Trunk R.R. Station.

Above: Postcard of Grand Trunk Railway station, India Street, Portland. *Author collection.*

Left: Grand Trunk Railway station, Poland's Corner, Cumberland. *Courtesy of Cumberland Historical Society.*

United States during the Civil War and for years after as well, having built up a reputation for producing high-quality textiles.

Textiles became more and more in demand following the Civil War, and to meet the shipping needs of the textile mills in Lewiston, a spur was built to connect to the Grand Trunk in Danville Junction (Auburn) from Lewiston. The Grand Trunk Railway spur was built in 1874 by the Lewiston and Auburn Railroad Company and leased to the Grand Trunk Railway.

Because of this, Lewiston transformed from a small farming community into a bustling mill town. The booming mills needed workers, and the railroad was the conduit for many to come. The majority of the needed textile workers were French-Canadians who emigrated from Quebec, Canada, through the Grand Trunk Railway in Lewiston to find work. The Lewiston station still exists at the corner of Lincoln and Beech Streets.

Trackside view of Grand Trunk Railway station, Lewiston. *Author photo.*

While a great deal was going on in Lewiston with the Grand Trunk Railway, much more was going on forty miles away in Portland. The railway had four different major locations in Portland: the first where the headquarters and train station was located; the second across the street where the wharves were built on Casco Bay; the third west of the headquarters and wharves where the grain elevators were built; and the fourth the engine and train car maintenance facility farther inland on Presumpscot Street.

The headquarters and railway station were on India Street, and docks and wharves were built almost directly across the street from these buildings, making it easy for passengers arriving by train to simply walk across the street and board the steamships and for passengers arriving from the steamships to cross the street, walk up to the train station and board trains departing from there. Freight arriving on trains was unloaded on the tracks between the headquarters building and docks and then loaded onto ships, and freight arriving on the ships was transloaded onto trains at that location as well. This was a very efficient operation for the handling of both passengers and freight by the Grand Trunk Railway.

Portland was the southern terminus of the key Grand Trunk line running from Montreal to the coast of Maine. To create more loading capability on Portland's waterfront, the Grand Trunk Railway needed more docks and wharves as close as possible to the headquarters building, the train station and the tracks across the street, which were right on the Casco Bay shoreline. To accomplish this, it purchased land from the famous poet and Portland resident Henry Wadsworth Longfellow. The waterfrontage sold by Longfellow was across from the Grand Trunk Railway headquarters and is today the Franklin Street Wharf where the Maine State Pier (Portland Ocean Terminal) and the Ocean Gateway Terminal for cruise ships docking at Portland now stand.

The Grand Trunk headquarters building on the corner of India and Commercial Streets was completed in 1903. This building housed offices not only for Grand Trunk railroad operations but for two transatlantic steamship companies as well. Gorham Savings Bank purchased and rehabilitated this building in 2016 to use as corporate offices, ensuring this historic site will be preserved for decades to come.

Most of the rail activity in Portland revolved around exporting agricultural goods to Europe and importing freight from Europe. The Grand Trunk Railway was instrumental in making this happen. Grain was arriving in Portland by rail from interior Maine and Canada, so grain storage was needed until it could be loaded on ships for delivery to Liverpool, England. Huge grain elevators were built about two miles west of the wharves to hold this grain.

Grand Trunk and Steamship offices, India Street, Portland. *Author photo*.

The fourth area in Portland for the Grand Trunk Railway was home to a very large maintenance facility and roundhouse about three miles farther north from the waterfront on Presumpscot Street to service engines and repair freight and passenger rail cars. A roundhouse is a turntable where heavy engines can be turned around to enter maintenance bays for servicing and repair. Once the repairs are completed, the engines can leave the maintenance bay, turn around and leave the facility.

A branch of the Maine Bureau of Motor Vehicles is now located in the roundhouse office building. Engines from all the Grand Trunk Railway lines were brought to this maintenance for major repairs.

Two transatlantic steamship companies, eventually headquartered in the Grand Trunk headquarters, also began operating out of the port of Portland. These steamships performed the same function as cruise ships do today. The first steamship to begin operations was the British and North American Royal Main Steam-Packet Company, which became the Cunard Steamship Company, Ltd., and finally named the Cunard Line in 1878. The British and North American Royal Main Steam-Packet Company was the brainchild of Samuel Cunard, a Halifax, Nova Scotia shipowner who was awarded the first British transatlantic steamship main contract in 1839. The next year, he formed the British and North American Royal Mail Steam-Packet Company.

The second transatlantic steamship company carrying passengers between Portland, Maine, and Liverpool, England, was the White Star–Dominion Line.

Both of these steamship lines later had offices in the Grand Trunk headquarters building on the corner of India and Commercial Streets in Portland. If you look again at the photo of the headquarters building, you will notice it says, "Grand Trunk and Steamship Offices." This historic headquarters building still stands today, but sadly, the Grand Trunk station itself was demolished in 1961, a victim of urban renewal.

The demise of shipping freight and carrying passengers via rail from Montreal to Portland began when icebreaker ships were built in the 1930s and were used to clear the St. Lawrence River of two-foot-thick ice. From that point, freight could be shipped directly to Europe from the Port of Montreal, and passenger cruise ships could sail directly from there as well.

Demand for wharf space for cruise ships in Portland has grown exponentially over the past twenty years as the port of Portland is once again becoming more and more a desired destination for cruise ships. More than four hundred cruise ships carrying more than 380,000 passengers visited Portland in 2017.

Chapter 8

BANGOR AND AROOSTOOK RAILROAD

The Bangor and Aroostook Railroad (BAR) was the railroad company that brought rail service to Aroostook County in northern Maine. The BAR rolling stock boxcars were easily recognizable throughout the United States in the 1950s because of their brightly painted exterior.

The Bangor and Aroostook Railroad began in 1891 by combining the former Bangor and Piscataquis Railroad and the Bangor and Katahdin Iron Works Railroad. The line extended from Bangor, where it was based, to Oakfield and Houlton in 1894 and farther in 1895 to Fort Fairfield and Caribou. In 1896, a line was extended from Oakfield to Ashland, and another branch was built from Caribou to Limestone in 1897. The Ashland branch was extended to Fort Kent in 1902. A southern line was constructed in 1905, connecting at the Northern Maine Junction to Searsport on Penobscot Bay.

More expansion was on the way as the Bangor and Aroostook Railroad built the "Medford Cutoff" from Packard to South Lagrange in 1907 and a branch was built from Millinocket to a new paper mill in East Millinocket. Rail lines were further extended from Van Buren to Madawaska and Fort Kent to St. Francis in 1910. Mapleton, Stockholm and Presque Isle were on the main line.

In the early 1900s, the Bangor and Aroostook Railroad began shipping chemicals and logs to the paper mills and shipping finished paper and pulp out from the mills located along the Penobscot River at Millinocket and East

Bangor and Aroostook Railroad engine #142. *Maine Historical Society Item #10445, Collections of Oakfield Historical Society.*

Millinocket. A paper mill was built in Madawaska in 1925 that was serviced by the BAR. Pulpwood and wood chips were now being shipped into the mills via rail from within Aroostook County in Maine and from Canada via the International Railroad Bridge.

A critical connection was needed for carrying potatoes and other products from Aroostook County to ports in Canada and for carrying products and raw materials from Canada to mills and farmers in Aroostook County. To meet this need, an international bridge was constructed over the St. John River between Van Buren and St. Leonard, New Brunswick, Canada, in 1915 to connect with the Canadian Pacific Railway and the National Transcontinental Railway. The Canadian Pacific Railway and the National Transcontinental Railway later merged to become the Canadian National Railway.

Hauling potatoes was the BAR's most profitable endeavor from 1895, when it put the heated boxcars into service, through the Great Depression. These BAR boxcars were insulated and heated with special stoves to keep the potatoes they were carrying from freezing in the winter. These boxcars carried paper products the rest of the year.

The Bangor and Aroostook Railroad had an arrangement with the Penn Central (PC) Railroad to take the BAR heated boxcars at Selkirk Yard in

State of Maine boxcar model train on display at Boothbay Railway Village. *Author photo.*

New York State, hook the cars to its engines and take them to destinations south and west. During the winter of 1969–70, Penn Central's interchange service became untenable. It didn't keep the boxcar heaters fueled, so a large portion of the 1969 potato crop from Aroostook County was spoiled by freezing. The Bangor and Aroostook Railroad and Aroostook County potato farmers filed claims against the Penn Central Transportation Company, but the following year, PC filed for bankruptcy, leaving both the Bangor and Aroostook Railroad and the farmers without recourse. Several large potato farms went out of business as a result, and the remaining farmers didn't have faith in the BAR and began shipping their potato crops by truck. Trucks began transporting potatoes when the interstate highway system came to northern Maine in the 1960s, causing the BAR to lose a lot of its most profitable business.

More than 50 percent of BAR's revenues was from hauling potatoes following World War II. During the 1950s, the Bangor and Aroostook Railroad was second only to the Santa Fe Railroad for refrigerated boxcars (reefers) designed specifically to be cooled with ice in the summer to prevent potatoes from spoiling. The BAR had icing stations located in Houlton, Presque Isle and Caribou. The Bangor and Aroostook worked out an arrangement with the Pacific Fruit Express (PFE), based in California, in the 1950s in which the PFE shipped Maine potatoes during winter months and the BAR transported California produce during the summer and fall.

Bangor and Aroostook Railroad refrigerated boxcar ("Ice Reefer"), 7187, loading potatoes from Aroostook County onto the SS *Pioneer Dale* ship at Port of Searsport, 1965. *Maine Historical Society Item #17836, Collections of Oakfield Historical Society.*

The PFE was a joint venture leasing company formed by the Union Pacific Railroad and the Southern Pacific Railroad consisting of 6,600 refrigerated boxcars. The PFE is still in operation today but totally owned by the Union Pacific Railroad.

The Bangor and Aroostook also had another advantage, and that was to use the port of Searsport to ship timber, potatoes and other products around the world by ship and by importing the coal it needed for its locomotives from that port without having to negotiate joint rates with the Maine Central Railroad. Prior to the use of this port, the BAR had to pay MEC to transport shipments over its rail lines from Bangor south. By 1927, the BAR handled more than thirty-two thousand cars of potatoes, 30 percent of its total freight tonnage. About 23 percent represented forest products, and 14 percent was for transporting paper.

The rail connection at the port of Searsport also became critical in World War II for bringing in ammunitions and explosives by train and loading them onto ships at the port of Searsport. The army considered Searsport the preferred loading point for ammunition brought by train to be loaded onto ships going to Europe. During World War II, 435,353 tons of army-procured ammunition and high explosives shipped overseas from Searsport from December 1941 to August 1945. All of these munitions were transported by rail by a mutual connection agreement between the Bangor and Aroostook Railroad and the Maine Central Railroad. Moreover, the BAR transported heating coal, munitions and aircraft to Loring Air Force Base, near Limestone, for the B-52 bombers of the Strategic Air Command through the Cold War.

Iron Road Railways acquired the BAR in 1995. The company went bankrupt in 2002, and its lines were sold to Rail World, Inc., which incorporated them into the newly formed Montreal, Maine and Atlantic Railway.

Chapter 9

THE MONTREAL, MAINE
AND ATLANTIC RAILWAY
(CENTRAL MAINE AND QUEBEC RAILWAY)

T he Montreal, Maine and Atlantic (MM&A) Railway operated
from 2003 to 2014. Its primary business was hauling potatoes
and timber products, like pulp and paper. In 2003, the first year
of MM&A's operation, the railroad operated over 745 miles of track and
dispatched twenty-five trains a day. During its last few years, it was operating
over only about 500 miles of track and the number of trains dispatched
was only about ten to twelve per day, resulting in lower and lower profits.
Because of lower profits, MM&A was spending less in the maintenance and
repair of the tracks, especially along the northern routes from Millinocket
to Madawaska.

Railroads across the United States were struggling in the 1990s and
2000s. Many only stayed profitable through mergers and acquisitions.
Simply put, trucking products was becoming more and more preferred
by shippers. Congress was taking notice and doing what it could to keep
the railroads operational. This was significantly important for a large rural
state, like Maine. Maine's U.S. representative, John Baldacci, understood the
impact that losing rail service to northern Maine would have on farmers,
paper mills and other businesses in that area. Without rail service, many
Aroostook County farmers and businesses wouldn't be able to survive; they
simply couldn't compete with shipping via trucks. Congressman Baldacci
served Maine on the Transportation Committee and on the Subcommittee
on Railroads during his tenure in Congress from 1995 to 2003, and he was

focused on doing whatever he could to keep freight moving on the railroads and restore passenger travel by train.

During Baldacci's two terms as Maine's governor, Maine's unemployment rate rose to more than 8 percent and the economy was struggling, going through the deepest recession since the Great Depression. As a result of the sluggish economy, state revenues were also flat. But he again recognized that bold action needed to be taken to not only save the farmers, paper mills and other businesses in Maine but help them grow as well. Governor Baldacci was acutely aware that shipping by rail was changing. Shipping via rail had evolved from transporting a lot of different products to mostly carrying lumber, paper and pulp products, logs and wood chips out of northern Maine to now bringing in cooking oil for French fry plants, fertilizer, propane, chemicals and heating oil in Aroostook County.

By 2009, the Montreal, Maine and Atlantic Railway was losing $4 million to $5 million annually. MM&A notified the federal Surface and Transportation Board that the railroad lines from Millinocket north to Madawaska were the main cause of the loss of profits and they intended to abandon these 233 miles of track. These are the same lines that MM&A had been neglecting to maintain and repair for several years. Governor Baldacci was aware that the more than two dozen businesses in Aroostook County that used the trains as a cost-effective shipping alternative to trucks were at immediate risk of going out of business and many more businesses would likely be adversely affected or even put out of business if rail service was discontinued.

Governor Baldacci came to office in 2003 understanding these challenges, and he immediately set to work with the state legislature on a progressive policy to not only keep the railroad operating to northern Maine but also work to restore passenger travel in Maine. From the start of his governorship, he had a plan ready to implement. First, he had to stop the planned abandonment of these rail lines. Working closely with legislative leaders and with David Cole (his transportation commissioner), Bruce Van Note (the deputy commissioner) and their team, the state agreed to purchase the 233 miles of track from Millinocket to the Canadian border for $20 million. The money included $7 million from state reserve accounts, $7 million from a 2010 bond issue, $4 million from a 2009 bond issue, $1.1 million in unused state transportation funds that had been earmarked for rail projects and $1 million from Irving Woodlands, a major shipper on the line. Irving Woodlands owned more than 1.5 million acres of forest land, making it the largest Maine private landowner. This forest land was where most of the logs came from to supply the paper mills all over the state of Maine. Buying these rail lines was only one part of the solution, however. Baldacci also had to find the money to repair and maintain the railroad. Working with Maine's senior senator, Olympia Snowe, who served on the Senate Finance Committee, and the Obama administration, he obtained a $10.5 million grant for this purpose. Finally, the governor also had to find a railroad company to operate a railroad along these tracks. The state negotiated an agreement for operating rights to Irving's Maine Northern Railway (MNRY). This short-line railroad is owned by the New Brunswick (Canada) Railway Company, a holding company that is part of Irving Transportation Services, a division of J.D. Irving, Ltd. MNRY agreed to operate these 233 miles of track in Maine from Millinocket to Madawaska. This enabled MNRY to interconnect with two of its sister companies, the New Brunswick Southern Railway (NBSR) and Eastern Maine Railway (EMRY), which operate 190 miles connecting the major shipping port of St. John, New Brunswick (Canada), to Brownville Junction, near Milo, Maine, where the railroad connected to other railroads south to Bangor and beyond. It could arguably be stated that Governor John Baldacci and his administration saved the railroads north of Millinocket and the livelihood of many large farmers and other businesses in Aroostook County.

The portion of the tracks from the Millinocket and East Millinocket paper mills to the port of Searsport was still very profitable, however. So MM&A continued to operate this one-hundred-mile railroad line.

A great tragedy occurred in 2013, when a major derailment involving the MM&A occurred at Lac-Megantic, a town in Quebec twenty-two miles from the U.S. border. At approximately 1:15 a.m. on July 6, 2013, an unattended seventy-four-car freight train carrying crude oil in rail tank cars rolled down a 1.2 percent grade from Nantes, a nearby town, and derailed in downtown Lac-Megantic, resulting in a massive fire and explosion of several of the tank cars carrying the oil. A rail tank car carries about 30,000 gallons of crude oil, so more than 1.5 million gallons of crude oil was on this train. Trains carrying crude oil are required to be attended at all times for safety purposes. Forty-two people died in the disaster, and five more were missing and presumed dead. More than thirty buildings in the town center were destroyed, and of the thirty-nine remaining buildings, all but three were contaminated so badly from the oil that they, too, had to be demolished. Building damages were reported within a half-mile radius of the explosion downtown.

The MM&A never recovered from this disaster financially and went bankrupt in 2013. The line assets were sold to Fortress Investments and continue today as the Central Maine and Quebec (CMQ) Railway. The CMQ is headquartered in Bangor. CMQ also has a full-service rail car repair facility in Derby, near Milo, and track repair facilities in Farnham, Quebec, and rail car storage areas. Farnham is about forty miles east of Montreal and about sixty-five miles north of Burlington, Vermont.

Today, Central Maine and Quebec Railway operates 492 miles of track delivering freight throughout Maine, Vermont and Quebec and to points beyond through its interchanges with Canadian National Railway, Canadian Pacific Railway, CSX Transportation (Railroad), Norfolk Southern Railway, New Brunswick Central Railway, Maine Northern Railway, Vermont Railway, Pan Am Southern and the St. Lawrence and Atlantic Railroad.

Chapter 10

MAINE CENTRAL RAILROAD

We've read about how the Boston and Maine Railroad connected Boston with Portland and how the St. Lawrence and Atlantic Railroad and the Grand Trunk Railway connected Portland to Montreal. So now we will look at how the Maine Central Railroad connected Portland to Bangor and on to New Brunswick, Canada. The Maine Central Railroad began in the mid-nineteenth century by purchasing smaller short-line railroads that were transporting large amounts of logs and lumber to and from mills located farther inland to coastal ports in Maine, then to be transported to other ports in the United States and abroad. There were numerous small railroad companies that were hauling logs and lumber, and the need was growing exponentially, as was the competition. On October 28, 1862, many of these smaller railroads merged to form the Maine Central Railroad. (See appendix III for railroads in Maine that became part of the Maine Central Railroad Company.) The railroad continued to expand and prosper through the leasing and purchasing of rail lines. The Canadian Pacific Railroad operated the section of the line that ran from St. John, New Brunswick, across the St. Croix–Vanceboro Railway Bridge to Vanceboro, Maine, and the Maine Central operated the 163 miles of line from Vanceboro to Bangor.

It traveled northeast from Portland to Vanceboro, where it crossed the St. Croix River via the St. Croix–Vanceboro Railway Bridge to connect with the New Brunswick Southern Railway in St. Croix. The Canadian government referred to the St. Croix–Vanceboro Railway Bridge as the McAdam Bridge,

Left: Union Station, Bangor. *Courtesy Bangor Public Library*.

Below: Cumberland Center Depot, 1934. *Courtesy Cumberland Historical Society*.

named for the large municipality east of the town of St. Croix. The bridge was jointly owned by the Canadian Pacific Railroad on the Canadian side and the Maine Central Railroad on the U.S. side.

A very historical event took place when an attempt was made by an Imperial German spy to blow up this bridge on February 2, 1915. The United States was still neutral in World War I, but Canada had entered the war in support of Britain in 1914. Japan had also entered the war in support of Britain in 1914, and Germany feared that Japan might send troops across the Pacific Ocean and through Canada to join British forces on the

German lieutenant Werner Horn (*left*) with Washington County deputy George Ross. *Courtesy St. Croix Historical Society.*

western front of the war. The German government was convinced that would occur and ordered that the Canadian railway system be interrupted. The bombing plans were masterminded by Franz von Papen, the military attaché of the German Embassy in Washington, D.C., at the time and the bombing was executed by Lieutenant Werner Horn, a ten-year German army veteran solicited to place the bomb. The bomb failed to destroy the bridge but made it unsafe to use until minor repairs were done. The explosion did, however, blow out windows in nearby buildings in St. Croix and Vanceboro. Von Papen served later as chancellor of Germany in 1932 and vice-chancellor of Germany under Adolf Hitler in 1933–34. Since the United States was neutral at the time of the bombing, Lieutenant Horn could move freely throughout the country. Huge quantities of military supplies and troops were moving through Canada via the Canadian Pacific Railroad and through Maine via the Maine Central Railroad. German planners determined an easily accessible weak link along this route was the railroad bridge at Vanceboro, Maine.

Just before midnight on February 1, 1915, Horn checked out of the hotel he was staying at in Vanceboro, changed into his German army uniform so he wouldn't be convicted and executed as a spy if caught and, carrying a suitcase filled with explosives, placed the bomb on a girder on the bridge.

Horn lit the fuse with a cigar and hurried back so he wouldn't be placed at the scene of the bombing when the bomb went off. The bomb only bent some iron beams and the damage was minor; the bridge was fully operational after repairs in less than a week.

Early the next morning, the superintendent of the Maine Central Railroad, accompanied by a posse of locals, arrested Horn without resistance. He admitted he placed the bomb but claimed he was justified as an officer in the Germany army to attack the enemy. He emphasized that he placed the bomb on the Canadian side of the bridge and Canada was at war with Germany.

Britain wanted Horn to be extradited to face trial, but the United States refused the extradition request and tried and sentenced him to prison in the United States. He served a few years in a U.S. prison, and after his release, he was extradited to Canada, where he was tried, convicted and received a ten-year sentence to be served at the Dorchester Prison in New Brunswick. In 1921, he was declared insane and returned to Germany.

In 1925, the Maine Central Railroad was promoting travel by train. Here is what it had to say in the December 1925 edition of *Maine Central Employees* magazine:

> *As yet the folks of Maine haven't come to a thorough appreciation of what this train (*The Pine Tree Limited*) means, but they are waking to it. Each day sees an increase in patronage. Men are finding that for them to go to Portland to transact business is made much easier by patronizing this train. The Waterville man who desires can leave that city at 5:20 in the morning, go to Portland, have two hours for business and be back at three in the afternoon. He can go to Boston, have five hours and be home at 9:30 in the evening. A Lewiston man doesn't have to leave home until an hour later than his Waterville friend, and be home correspondingly early. Augusta, Gardiner, Richmond, and Bowdoinham and Brunswick people benefit proportionately.*

Extending railroads to parts of Maine was challenging at times due to Maine's geography. To get passenger, freight and locomotives across the mouth of the Kennebec River prior to 1927, they had to use ferries because a bridge didn't exist. In 1871, ferries carried train cars across the Kennebec River to the Knox and Lincoln Railroad so trains could go farther up the coast to Rockland. The *City of Rockland* and the *Hercules* were the first train ferries, but they could transport only passenger and freight cars. In 1909, the train ferry *Fernando Gorges* was added, allowing locomotives to also cross the river.

These ferries continued to operate until the Carlton Bridge opened on October 25, 1927. Train ferries were no longer needed. The first two trains crossed the bridge that day carrying 2,500 passengers, with 880 of them coming from Rockland and other places along the Knox and Lincoln branch to take part in the celebration.

The Carlton Bridge is a railroad vertical-lift bridge that carries one track over the Kennebec River. Until August 1, 2000, it also carried two lanes of U.S. Route 1 on its upper deck, after which the highway was transferred to the Sagadahoc Bridge, a new highway bridge adjacent to the Carlton Bridge. With the removal of U.S. 1 from the Carlton Bridge, its primary traffic is freight trains bound for manufacturers in Thomaston.

While freight was the bulk of the business of the Maine Central Railroad, the railroad also led the way in developing Maine as a vacation and holiday destination. Vacationers from as far away as southern New England, New Jersey and New York City began to choose Maine as their desired vacation spot. The Maine Central Railroad added luxurious parlor cars and coaches to take vacationers to luxury hotels. The railroad also purchased a fleet of steamships, extending the reach of vacationers well beyond the rail lines. A

Carlton Bridge, Bath, Maine, 1935. *Maine Historical Society Item #66287, Collections of Boston Public Library.*

major lease by the Maine Central Railroad involved connecting transatlantic cruise ships between Halifax and St. John, Canada, and New York City.

By the early twentieth century, the Maine Central Railroad owned or leased more than 1,500 miles of rail lines. The Maine Central Railroad and other railroads throughout Maine, like the Grand Trunk Railway, connected rural towns in eastern Maine with larger communities like Bangor, which created more opportunities for economic development. One of the Maine Central Railroad's biggest customers was transporting logs to the many paper mills that cropped up along the rivers and rail lines. At its peak in the 1930s, the company had seventy-eight locomotives in service and was transporting more than one million passengers as well.

After World War II, Maine Central Railroad ramped up its investment in train tracks and railroad cars to handle an increasing demand for passenger service by adding modern streamlined coaches and elaborate dining cars and by creating high-speed round trips for passengers between Bangor and Boston. But the profits from passenger service fell dramatically by 1950 as a result of more and more use of automobiles, and the railroad sold off some of its lines of track throughout Maine. The Maine Central Railroad created the Maine Central Transportation Company, a bus company, to take advantage of those who wanted to travel directly to towns that weren't on the railroad line. These buses complemented passenger travel via train, not competing directly with it. These buses also carried mail to the small towns along their routes.

A major event, Hurricane Edna, in 1954 dealt a devasting blow to the Maine Central Railroad. It was one of the worst storms to hit Maine, and the hurricane stopped the railroad from operating. Hundreds of miles of track were washed out and profits plummeted due to the loss of freight and passenger travel. The costs to repair the damage caused by the hurricane were enormous, so in order for the railroad to survive, the company immediately sold off the Maine Central Transportation Company, its bus service, to the Greyhound Bus Company.

By 1956, the losses from the railroad's passenger service were so bad that Maine Central discontinued the Farmington line in 1957 and eliminated the Bangor-Calais train that year as well. By 1958, the Maine Central Railroad had terminated all passenger service in Maine.

By the 1960s, most railroads in the United States had ceased passenger service completely and now had to rely only on hauling freight, which was not as profitable either with more and more freight being hauled by trucks. Moreover, the building of the interstate highway system made it easier for

Maine Central drawbridge and river front, Bangor. *Courtesy Bangor Public Library.*

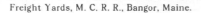

Freight yards, Maine Central Railroad, Bangor. *Courtesy Bangor Public Library.*

trucking companies to take more freight from the railroad. Trucks had an advantage, as they could transport freight door to door, whereas freight on rail cars had to be transloaded onto trucks from train depots to the customer. But a savior came along. At that time, the International Paper Company constructed the new Androscoggin Pulp and Paper Mill in Jay, and before long, this mill and other paper company mills in Maine became the railroads' largest customers, returning the Maine Central Railroad to a very profitable railroad once again. But the profitability didn't last long, and by the mid-1960s, the Maine Central Railroad was again seeing costs exceeding income. The railroad had to sell many of its branch lines; it simply had a hard time competing with over-the-road trucking.

The Maine Central Railroad had a resurgence once again when it started transporting potatoes and other crops, logs, wood products, coal, fuel oils, gasoline, newsprint/paper, gravel and textiles and leather goods, and by the early 1970s, it was making huge profits again hauling freight. Its profits in 1974 were the highest in the company's history. The company continued to carry a huge debt load, however, and ended up abandoning miles and miles of rail lines that were no longer profitable. Included in this was the abandonment of the fifty-plus-mile line from Quebec Junction, New Hampshire, to Beecher Falls, Vermont, which was one of its most profitable lines at one time. It also abandoned the Farmington Branch, and a couple of years later, it abandoned the line from North Anson to Bingham. The Eastport Branch was abandoned in 1978.

The strategy of the Maine Central Railroad in the late 1970s and through the 1980s was to regain prominence through mergers and more consolidation of existing rail lines. One of the creative ways the Maine Central Railroad remained profitable during this period was to make work with connecting railroads to eliminate the duplication of services, lower freight rates and pool maintenance services. This was a very bold, but very effective, strategy for the times.

The Maine Central Railroad company is in operation today as part of Pan Am Railways, which was once referred to as Guilford Transportation. It is still a very profitable railroad, hauling thousands of tons of freight each year. A critical operation for Pan Am Railways is the Portland Terminal Company (PTM) in South Portland, Maine. PTM began in 1911 to provide switching operations to and from Portland and for short lines to industries in and around Portland as well. PTM served as the junction of the Maine Central Railroad, the Boston and Maine Railroad and ·the Grand Trunk Railway. In 1981, Guilford Transportation Industries (GTI) bought the

Maine Central Railroad and the Boston and Maine Railroad. In 2006, the company renamed itself Pan Am Railways (PAR). The Grand Trunk Railway of Canada also served the northeast part of Portland. Today, the Grand Trunk Railway trackage is owned and operated by the St. Lawrence and Atlantic, a short-line subsidiary of Genesee and Wyoming Inc.

Portland Terminal includes Rigby Yard, which is over one and a half miles long and has a half parallel ladder track. There are numerous industrial spurs throughout the area serving distribution warehouses, intermodal facilities, other miscellaneous industries and oil terminals.

Rigby Yard was the base of the Maine Central Railroad and the interchange with the Boston and Maine Railroad. It was built in 1923 on the site of a former horse racing track. By the 1980s, 75,000 cars a year were coming into Rigby Yard. Maine Central and Boston and Maine freight trains all originated or terminated in Rigby Yard. Several local short rail lines connected the Rigby Yard to local businesses, for example, the New England Shipbuilding Corporation, the Portland-Montreal Pipe Line Terminal, the petroleum bulk plants in South Portland, a major grocery distribution facility in Deering Junction in Portland and other light industries. A major rail connection was to the S.D. Warren Paper Mill in Westbrook; in 1973, 7,500 carloads originated or terminated in Westbrook from Rigby Yard.

The Portland Terminal Company was a subsidiary of the Maine Central Railroad with its own foundry shops on Thompson Point in Portland and had tracks from there to Rigby Yard. This facility still stands near the Amtrak station there. The Thompson Point shops built forty-nine flatcars, forty boxcars, three cabooses, one baggage–railway post office car (RPO) and one RPO-smoking car for the two-foot Bridgton and Saco River Railroad and the Sandy River and Rangeley Lakes Railroad between 1912 and 1917.

Chapter 11

GUILFORD TRANSPORTATION/PAN AM RAILWAYS

Guilford Transportation Company (GTI) became a major player in carrying freight throughout the Northeast United States when it entered the railroad business in 1981. It bought not only the Maine Central Railroad but also the Boston and Maine Corporation and the Delaware and Hudson Railway Company. In 1998, GTI purchased the name, colors and logo of Pan American World Airways. GTI changed its name to Pan Am Systems in 2006. The company is privately owned by an heir to the Mellon banking fortune, Timothy Mellon, and other stakeholders, including David Fink, formerly of Penn Central, and his son, David A. Fink.

GTI's strategy was to create efficiencies by improving freight car utilization, consolidating management and equipment and creating run-through train services to ultimately offer lower freight costs than independent railroads. Run-through trains ensure compatible infrastructure throughout the system. This was accomplished by ensuring that rolling stock dimensions, curve speed and signaling compatibility, train dimensions, tunnel and bridge dimensions and maximum weight and power requirements were compatible with all equipment throughout the system.

Guilford Transportation did all of this because it had projected an increasing demand in economic activity in this area of the United States. The company now either owned or leased more than four thousand miles of rail lines, stretching from Montreal, Canada, to Washington, D.C., and from Calais, Maine, to Buffalo, New York. With a combined workforce of about 4,500 employees and with approximately four hundred locomotives

Pan Am Railways/Guilford Transportation engines at Rigby Yard, South Portland. *Author photo.*

and twelve thousand freight cars, the new system resulted in an improved opportunity to haul and route more freight more easily than ever before. Guilford Transportation achieved its intended goals, attracting significant new traffic each year. By 1996, it had established a strong presence hauling freight. It survived challenges to the industry brought on by deregulation because of its earlier strategies, and profits continued even in competing with trucks hauling more and more freight. This occurred, in part, by working with the trucking industry to "piggyback" trucks and containers.

Pan Am also owns Perma Treat Corporation, which manufacturers railroad ties and other pressure-treated products at facilities in Mattawamkeag, Maine, and Durham, Connecticut. Perma Treat recycles used railroad ties to generate electricity at the Aroostook and Bangor Resources Inc. facilities in Mattawamkeag.

The first few years of Guilford Transportation operating railroads in Maine were rough for the company, its workers and the companies that shipped by rail. GRI abandoned lines, leaving companies without a way to transport products by rail, and a lot of union unrest occurred, some resulting in strikes. Many employees felt treatment by GTI management was very harsh, and GTI's reputation was damaged as a result. The company was not very profitable, so it began cost-cutting measures by eliminating routes that were the least profitable or even operating at a loss. It laid off workers, closed shops and cut pay, resulting in the Brotherhood of Maintenance Way Employees striking in March 1986. The union, representing sixty-five workers, was protesting new work rules and a 20 percent wage cut. The strike ended after eighty-four days under a back-to-work order by President Ronald Reagan. On September 30, 1986, President Reagan signed legislation imposing a settlement to avoid disrupting rail transportation nationwide. The settlement required Guilford Industries to increase track workers' wages by 6.5 percent by July 1988 and to make severance payments of up to $26,000 each to more than fifty workers laid off since the March 3 strike began. Guilford officials said the company lost $11 million in the first seven months of 1986, mostly due to the strike.

GTI's intent was to apply to come under the rules for a short-line railroad under the Association of American Rules as defined by the federal Standard Transportation Board. Short-line railroads are considered Class III railroads applying revenue standards. Railroads are classified by total revenue. Here are the classifications by revenue for railroads as of 2017:

> *Class I railroads are regulated by the STB and subject to the Uniform System of Accounts (49 CFR 1201). These carriers are also required to file annual and periodic financial and statistical reports. Railroads are classified based on their annual operating revenues. The class to which a carrier belongs is determined in accordance with the following revenue thresholds:*
> - *Class I—$447,621,226 or more*
> - *Class II—Less than $447,621,226 but in excess of $35,809,698*
> - *Class III—$35,809,698 or less*

These revenue thresholds are periodically updated to account for the impact of inflation. They were last updated in 2017.

Moving to a lower class of railroad would enable GTI/Pan Am to pay workers using a lower wage scale and would give the company more flexible work rules, resulting in less pay and fewer benefits. The *Philadelphia Inquirer* commented in an article about this titled "An Investor Believes He's on Track; Banking Heir Timothy D. Mellon Has Poured Millions into Regional Railroads: He's Also Stirred Controversy." The paper reported that Guilford Transportation had "become the bane of organized labor for a harsh, confrontational approach to trimming costs." Most railroad executives dismissed Mellon as a wealthy heir who suffered from gross mismanagement, possessed a willful misunderstanding of the inner workings of a railroad and was a "stubborn ideologue."

Guilford Transportation's growth remained flat, arguably due to poor management decisions by the company, except for a short spurt in the

1990s. After Guilford Transportation underwent the name change to Pan Am Railways, freight traffic dropped considerably. The Maine Department of Transportation (DOT) issued a report showing that prior to Guilford Transportation acquiring the other railroads, the amount of freight carried was much larger. In 1972, Maine DOT reported 162,658 loads on the Maine Central Railroad, one of the railroads acquired by Guilford Transportation. By 2008, traffic over the portions of the remaining lines of MEC now run by Pan Am was estimated at less than 69,000 loads—less than half of the loads carried in 1972. Railroad freight traffic throughout the United States, however, was estimated to have doubled over that same period. So while Pan Am freight traffic dropped, railroads across the United States were seeing an increase in business.

Pan Am has faced environmental issues as well. In March 2009, Pan Am was assessed the largest corporate criminal fine in Massachusetts history for failing to report a diesel fuel spill of hundreds of gallons near Ayer, Massachusetts. The company was also criticized as recently as 2017 for dumping railroad ties that contain creosote rather than disposing of them properly.

Guilford/Pan Am also resisted assisting Amtrak, which wanted to use the Guilford/Pan Am rail lines from Boston to Portland. The concerns Guilford/Pan Am had were surrounding equipment, weight limits and the speed for Amtrak trains. By December 1998, however, a speed limit of seventy-nine miles per hour was agreed to by both Guildford/Pan Am and Amtrak. The federal Surface Transportation Board (STB), which regulates and decides disputes involving railroad rates, mergers and other transportation matters, approved this agreement in 1999. Another issue arose following this agreement when Guilford/Pan Am refused to help with improving the tracks on that route, forcing the STB to get involved on Amtrak's behalf. Track upgrades were finally made in 2000 for Amtrak to begin service for its new Downeaster line in 2001. Again, Guilford/Pan Am delayed the start of the Amtrak service between Boston and Portland by refusing to allow Amtrak speeds in excess of fifty-nine miles per hour, even though the STB approved the seventy-nine-miles-per-hour speed limit over those tracks. Guilford/Pan Am also refused to allow Amtrak to operate test trains over its tracks. The STB notified Guildford/Pan Am that it was violating the agreements signed with Amtrak. The Downeaster finally began its service on December 14, 2001. It is important to note that Maine's governor at the time, John Baldacci, was instrumental in getting these issues resolved.

One of Governor Baldacci's positions when he came into office in 2003 was that rail was extremely important to the state, along with maintaining jobs, saving critical Maine shipping ports, alleviating traffic on Maine roads and trying to reduce air pollution. One goal the governor had was to have more and more transport by rail rather than by truck to decrease the amount of heavy truck traffic on Maine roads and decrease the emissions from trucks, as well. Shipping via rail is several times more energy-efficient than via trucks. Railroads move a ton of freight more than four hundred miles for each gallon of diesel fuel. A truck moves a ton of freight only about one hundred miles for each gallon of diesel fuel. Moreover, trucks emit three times as much pollution. So shipping via rail rather than by truck is cheaper, less polluting and lessens the damage of all the truck traffic deteriorating Maine roads. It is estimated that one train can remove the freight equivalent of 280 or more trucks off our roadways.

Soon after entering office, Governor Baldacci set goals to continue to support Maine's Three-Port Strategy developed in the 1970s, which encompassed the ports in Eastport, Searsport and Portland. He recognized that industrial port development was critical to expand shipping of Maine products via rail to these ports for shipment around the world.

Prior to 2003, more shipments originating in Maine left from Boston and other ports along the eastern coast than from ports in Maine. Governor Baldacci recognized the need for shippers in northern Maine to find cheaper ways to ship worldwide in order to keep farms and businesses operating and flourishing. He and his team were convinced that Portland was the answer to cutting hours and costs of transporting products from Aroostook County to Boston for shipping worldwide.

In 2003, Baldacci saw a new terminal completed at the port in Searsport as a result of a $20 million public/private partnership with Sprague Energy. Sprague is one of the largest independent suppliers of natural gas, heating oil, gasoline and diesel in Maine. Improvements were also made to the International Marine Terminal in Portland with the purchase of additional land and a new container crane, ensuring the Port of Portland would remain competitive. Because of Baldacci's foresight and aggressive actions, his successor was able to lure Eimskip, an international cargo container shipping company based in Iceland, to make Portland its cargo shipping hub. Eimskip has sixty-three offices in twenty countries and operates a twenty-two-ship fleet. The company is doing so well in Portland that it moved its U.S. headquarters to Portland from Virginia. Lumber from central and northern Maine and Canada comes via rail to Portland, where it is loaded onto ships for delivery worldwide. This is a huge advantage for Maine industries and

International Marine Terminal, Portland. *Author photo.*

businesses. The price is about the same to ship containers to Europe from Portland as it is to ship the same to the West Coast by rail or truck.

As of 2018, the volume of containers moving through the International Marine Terminal in Portland doubled from just five years earlier: 17,515 container units came through the port in 2018, more than double the 7,165 units recorded in 2013. The International Marine Terminal is Maine's only container terminal. More than $502.7 million in goods shipped through this terminal in 2018. Maine-made products—such as frozen cranberries and cranberry juice, frozen scallops, paperboard and bullet cartridges—are exported through the terminal, and frozen fish is imported for delivery to Maine.

Eimskip also leases containers to Poland Springs Water. Poland Springs now ships water in Eimskip containers via Pan Am to Ayer, Massachusetts, for transshipping across the United States. Starting in 2019, container shipments departed Portland to seven ports in Southeast Asia. Pan Am Railways transports the Eimskip containers from points in Maine and Canada to and from the International Marine Terminal in Portland.

While the early 2000s were at times contentious between Pan Am Railways and the state of Maine, Governor Baldacci's grit and determination kept the focus on doing what is best for Maine and ensuring Pan Am Railway's viability and success going forward by nurturing public/private partnerships and by keeping the State of Maine fully engaged in the process. As a result, Pan Am Railways is an important and vital part of the overall transportation needs for the citizens and businesses in the state of Maine.

Chapter 12

ELECTRIC RAILROADS IN MAINE

S ince the world first saw Thomas Davenport's model train in the 1830s, engineers have worked on using electric means to transport passengers. Trolleys, streetcars or "trams," as they are called in some parts of Europe, emerged as one of the first uses of electricity, along with the electric light.

TROLLEYS AND TRAMS

The trolley: a passenger vehicle powered by overhead wires, electrical rail system or horse.

A trolley pole is a tapered cylindrical pole of wood or metal used to transfer electricity from a "live" overhead wire to the control and the electric traction motors of a trolley or tram. The term "trolley" predates the invention of the trolley pole. The earliest electric cars did not use a pole but rather a system in which each car dragged behind it an overhead cable connected to a small cart—or "troller"—that rode on a "track" of overhead wires. From the side, the dragging lines made the car seem to be "trolling," like in fishing. Later, when a pole was added, it came to be known as a trolley pole.

The term *trolley* is also used to describe "the pole" or the passenger car using the trolley pole and is derived from the grooved conductive wheel (trolley) attached to the end of the pole that "trolls" the overhead wire.

The horse-drawn trolley was the first important step in trolley technology, as it demonstrated the great efficiency of steel wheels on tracks. Horse-drawn trolleys were in wide use prior to the 1800s and electricity. Electrical trolleys eliminated the problem of horse excrement and animal maintenance.

Most trolleys/trams use metal rails like a train on shared rights of way (on streets). Some trolleys are more of an electric bus with rubber tires, and they drive under catenaries (overhead wires) that supply electricity. You will find most trolleys or trams in dense urban or suburban areas. Tracks may be embedded in the street.

The majority of trolleys are supplied by overhead wires called catenaries. The group of wires has an upper strong wire in a curve (catenary) connected to a second wire below called a contact wire. The contract wire provides a smooth surface to follow for long overhead poles with conductors on the vehicle. Some devices don't use a pole device; they use a spring-like assembly called a pantograph. Trolleys use either an overhead cable or a "third rail" to supply power to an electric motor.

Early electric trolleys were vital to the growth of urban areas in the late 1800s. People would build residential neighborhoods along the trolley lines. Workers depended on trolleys to get to work on time. The trolley was a real moneymaker for all involved and, therefore, a good place to apply the new technology of electricity. For a brief time, the trolley was more important than electric lights because while only the wealthy in the late 1800s and early 1900s had electric lights in their homes, almost every blue-collar worker was riding the trolley to work.

Electric railways in Maine were very prevalent from the 1890s to the mid-1900s. More than ninety towns and cities in Maine had electric railways. Many of these trolleys operated only within the towns and cities, while others traveled short distances to places like the trolley parks and casinos in Old Orchard Beach, Brunswick and Portland and still others were interurban, traveling long distances between towns and cities. A few also carried freight as well as passengers, like the Aroostook Valley Railroad Company, which carried lumber, supplies and finished products to connect to larger railroads and on to New Hampshire, Massachusetts and beyond. In fact, more than five hundred miles of track was used for electric rails in Maine. This was at a time in our history when only 10 percent of those living in Maine had electricity in their homes! Trolley parks were developed by the trolley company owners to generate revenue on weekends when passengers didn't ride the trolleys to work. Citizens loved these trolley parks. They had merry-go-rounds for the children powered by motors similar to those used on the trolleys and grandstands where bands played. Moreover, the parks had electric lights so visitors could stay past dusk and ride the trolleys back home later in the evening.

Most of the electric railroads in Maine were about five to twenty miles long. The shortest electric rail service in Maine was the Norway and Paris Street Railway. It was only 2 miles long and carried only passengers. But a few had many more miles of track. The Portland Railroad was 83 miles long; the Atlantic Shore Railroad 90 miles long; and the Lewiston, Augusta and Waterville Railway had a whopping 152 miles of track. These electric railroads were interurban lines. The Portland-Lewiston Interurban (PLI) Railroad, although only 40 miles long, was one of the most popular and profitable electric rail lines in the early to mid-1900s. Interurban electric railroads were the precursor of the electric commuter rails we see today in major metropolitan areas.

Bangor Railway and Electric Company

The first electric railroad in Maine was operated by the Bangor Railway and Electric Company. This railroad was fifty-seven miles long, connecting Bangor, Brewer, Old Town, Orono, Hampden, Charleston, Winterport, Kenduskeag, Glenburn and Corinth. The railroad began just one year after the first electric trolley system in the country began operating in 1889. This area was the second in Maine to have steam locomotive trains and second in the country to have electric train service. John R. Graham was the man who made this happen. Graham was a successful businessman in Massachusetts. The General Electric Corporation, headquartered in Boston, had a large vested interest in an electric company in Bangor, the Public Works Company, that was failing. So the president of General Electric looked to Graham to lend his expertise to see if the Public Works Company could be made profitable. He asked Graham to travel to Bangor to investigate. Graham arrived in Bangor, investigated the company, made it profitable and saved it. He also saw that Bangor had a lot of other opportunities, primarily due to it being the closest port on Maine's largest river, the Penobscot, for loading large ships to carry agricultural goods and timber products from central and northern Maine around the world.

Graham decided to stay in Bangor. He moved there permanently and accepted the general manager and treasurer position for this failing utility, the Public Works Company. Within a few years, the company was

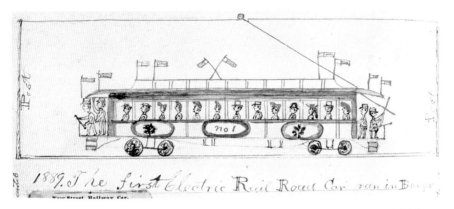

First electric car in Bangor, 1889. *Maine Historical Society Item #100952, Collections of Maine Historical Society and Maine State Museum.*

profitable, and he was able to raise enough capital to purchase the company. At that time, he formed the Bangor Railway and Electric Company, the immediate predecessor of Bangor Hydro-Electric Company, now called Emera Maine. This new company consolidated all the properties of the street railway, electric lighting and water departments of the Public Works Company, and it remained profitable from that point on. Then, Graham started building trolley lines throughout the Bangor region—trolley lines that would use electricity from the Public Works Company. The company now consisted of the Bangor Street Railway, the Old Town Electric Light and Power Company, the Penobscot Water and Power Company and the Brewer Water Company, as well as the Bangor, Orono and Old Town Railway and the Bangor and Northern and Bangor, Hampden and Winterport trolley lines.

This railway extended beyond the immediate Bangor area to neighboring towns to bring both passengers and freight to Bangor to connect with other railroads. A trolley bridge across the Penobscot River was built to connect Bangor's trolleys to Brewer's trolleys on the other side. This was a successful venture for many years, but by the 1920s, more and more people were choosing to use the automobile or buses rather than travel by electric rail. By 1931, the Charleston line ended. The Hampden line did by 1940 as well, and in 1941, the Old Town and Brewer line ended operations. By the mid-1940s, it was no longer feasible for the Bangor Railway and Electric Company to operate trolleys, so the company ceased trolley operations completely. The electric company division of the Bangor Railway and Electric Company still operates today.

AROOSTOOK VALLEY RAILROAD COMPANY

The only electric train service in northern Maine was the Aroostook Valley Railroad Company, which served Presque Isle, Washburn, Washburn Junction, New Sweden and Caribou. This railroad carried mostly potatoes— five thousand pounds in an average year—but also hay, fertilizer, grain, flour, starch, logs, lumber and some passengers. Passenger travel on the Aroostook Valley Railroad Company declined through the 1920s and 1930s, but the freight it hauled to interchange with the Bangor and Aroostook Railroad at Washburn and with the Canadian Pacific at Washburn Junction continued. In later years, heating oil and coal were brought into these towns and cities on the electric railroad, as was farm equipment. Military freight became a significant business during World War II, carrying eight to ten carloads per day to the air base in Presque Isle. The Presque Isle Air Force Base became the Skyway Industrial Park after the base closed in 1961. The Aroostook Valley Railroad, however, continued serving manufacturing facilities at the former air base. In the 1970s, manufacturers at Skyway Industrial Park and potato farmers began shipping by truck over the new Interstate 95 that was extended to Aroostook County in the late 1960s. The railroad ceased operations in 1996 when it was no longer profitable.

Aroostook Valley Railroad trestle, Canada, 1909. *Maine Historical Society Item #166322, Collections of Presque Isle Historical Society.*

Calais Street Railway car, St. Stephen, New Brunswick, Canada, 1900. The first international trolley traveled between Calais, Maine, and St. Stephen, New Brunswick, Canada. *Maine Historical Society Item #21153, Collections of St. Croix Historical Society.*

CALAIS STREET RAILWAY

Maine had an international electric railroad. The Calais Street Railway was seven miles long. It traveled in a loop across the St. Croix River from Calais, Maine, to St. Stephen, New Brunswick, Canada, and then traveled two miles upriver to Milltown, New Brunswick, where it crossed another bridge looping back to Calais in the United States. This was a passenger-only trolley; it didn't carry any freight.

The Calais Street Railway ended service on October 30, 1929, as more and more chose to travel by automobile.

PORTLAND RAILROAD

The Portland Railroad (PRR) had its beginning in the 1860s and ran continuously until May 1941. This was a huge company owning over two hundred electric railway passenger cars, also called trolleys, with more than ninety total miles of trackage. By 1903, the Portland Railroad system served Portland, South Portland, Cape Elizabeth, Scarborough, Saco, Old Orchard Beach, Westbrook, Gorham, South Windham, Falmouth, Cumberland and Yarmouth. It employed more than 500 workers at that time, including more than 125 motormen and a similar number of conductors. The motorman operates the trolley car. He is in charge of the motor of the electric car, much like a railroad engineer is in charge of the steam or diesel engine on modern trains. The conductor is responsible for about everything else, including overseeing the loading and unloading of freight/cargo, overseeing the safe and orderly transport of passengers, checking passenger tickets, taking payments from passengers, assisting passengers as necessary and announcing upcoming stations.

Monument Square—the junction of Congress, Preble, Middle, Federal and Elm Streets in downtown Portland—was the center of activity for this railway. All the trolley lines intersected here, and it was here that passengers could transfer to the Portland-Lewiston Interurban; the Biddeford and Saco Railroad; the Lewiston, Augusta and Waterville Railway; the Boston and Maine Railroad; the Maine Central Railroad; the Grand Trunk Railway; and the Casco Bay lines and other steamship companies that docked at the Portland wharves. Once arriving from the Portland Railroad trolley at Main Street in Saco, passengers could transfer to the Biddeford

Trolley at Dunstan Corner, Scarborough. *Maine Historical Society Item #29387, Collections of Scarborough Historical Society and Maine State Museum.*

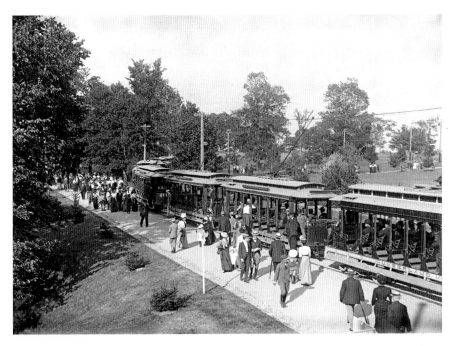

Boarding the trolley, Riverton Park, Portland. *Maine Historical Society Item #12164, Collections of Maine Historical Society.*

and Saco Railroad trolley to connect to the Atlantic Shore Line trolley system and travel to southern Maine and New Hampshire. The Portland Railroad ceased operations in May 1941 due to the popularity of travel by cars and buses.

Not all trolleys were urban; some trolleys, like the "bullet cars," had fewer stops, went between towns and evolved into what we now call "light rail."

Portland-Lewiston Interurban (PLI)

The Portland-Lewiston Interurban (PLI) electric railroad, a subsidiary of Androscoggin Electric Company, began operations in 1914, operating from Monument Square in Portland to Union Square in Lewiston. This was the first "express" train to operate in Maine, running hourly service over its single forty-mile track. The only stops it made along the way were in West Falmouth, Gray, New Gloucester, Upper Gloucester and Danville. At this time in Maine's railroad history, other trains serving this route made more stops along the way, taking about an hour and forty-five minutes to complete the run, while this new express train took only eighty minutes. This became the train of preference for those traveling between Maine's two largest cities.

The construction needed to build this railroad was significant and expensive. They had to build ten reinforced concrete bridges to handle the weight of the train spanning wide rivers. The span over the Presumpscot River, for example, was two hundred feet, and the span over the Little Androscoggin River in Auburn and another span near West Falmouth were both over one hundred feet. Androscoggin Electric had to negotiate an agreement with Portland, Lewiston and Auburn city streetcar lines before it could start construction. It accomplished this and began construction in June 1910. Thirty miles of seventy-pound steel rail in thirty-three-foot lengths had to be laid after obtaining private right-of-way rights along the route. The PLI built a siding in Gray so trains bound in different directions could pass. It took four years, but the Portland-Lewiston Interurban Railroad finally began service on July 7, 1914.

Just six weeks later, on August 14, former president Teddy Roosevelt rode the railroad from Portland to Gray, where he spoke from the back of the train to enthusiastic, cheering citizens. This event was captured by Ken Burns in his fourteen-hour documentary *The Roosevelts: An Intimate History*. While the United States had not yet entered World War I, Americans were very aware that it was inevitable. President Roosevelt was rallying Americans following the declaration of war by Austria-Hungary on Serbia on July 29, 1914. The United States entered the war later that year on December 8.

Most of the cars of the PLI were built by the Laconia Car Company, located in Laconia, New Hampshire, but a few were built by Wasson Manufacturing Company in Springfield, Massachusetts. The original four cars were forty-six feet long with a closed vestibule at either end. Each had six-foot smoking compartments and thirty-foot nonsmoking compartments. Both compartments had longitudinal seats. Each car was fitted with two power poles so the trains could operate in both directions. The cars had ninety horsepower motors to provide speeds up to fifty-nine miles per hour. Six of the luxury cars were named after flowers. One of PLI's passenger cars, the *Narcissus*, still exists today and can be seen at the Seashore Trolley Museum in Wells, Maine. It is undergoing major restoration to return it to its original state.

The Portland-Lewiston Interurban Railroad also hauled freight between the two cities. Some of the major shippers were dairy farmers shipping cans of raw milk to a milk processor in Portland. This was a very lucrative

Portland-Lewiston Interurban #14, *Narcissus*, in Gray, 1934. *Maine Historical Society Item #50686 Collections of Seashore Trolley Museum, Kennebunk.*

venture for the dairy farmers, the railroad and the milk processer as well. The cows could be milked, the raw milk canned and the cans loaded onto the southbound trains and arrive in Portland in less than one day. The box rail cars purposed for this were pulled by Baldwin Electric locomotives built in Eddystone, Pennsylvania. PLI also had ten flatcars that were used to transport cattle or bulky loads hauled by Baldwin Electric locomotives.

The power generated by the Androscoggin Electric Company for the railroad was hydroelectricity-generated by a dam between Lewiston and Auburn and by power from a steam power plant in Lewiston, when needed. Three-phase sixty-cycle power was transmitted to the Danville substation over the ten-thousand-volt lines used for residential and commercial use in Lewiston and Auburn. The electricity arriving at Danville was boosted to thirty-three-thousand-volt lines for more efficient transmission to the substations in Gray and Falmouth. Overhead catenary providing sixty-five-volt DC was supported by wooden poles at intervals of 120 feet. These poles also carried a separate telephone wire allowing continuous communication between trains and headquarters.

Androscoggin Electric merged with Central Maine Power in 1919. The Maine Statehood Centennial Exposition in Portland on July 5, 1920, created the heaviest passenger load on record for the PLI. A special coach smoker car, named *Maine*, was purchased for the exposition. There was so much demand during the Exposition that the PLI temporarily retrofitted box express cars with benches to carry all the passengers.

Automobiles were becoming more and more the desired mode of travel beginning in the 1920s, and that, coupled with the Great Depression, began the decline of rail travel. Interurban service ended on June 29, 1933, and all the tracks were pulled up in 1935. The Central Maine Power Company retained the Danville substation, but the Gray and West Falmouth substations were sold off and are now private residences. The Lewiston car barn was converted to a Red and White food store. A large portion of the right of way between Portland and West Falmouth is now part of the Maine Turnpike.

Atlantic Shore Line Railway

The story of the Atlantic Shore Line Railway, referred to as the Seaview Route, began with the merging of the Mousam River Railroad; the Sanford and Cape Porpoise Railway; the Portsmouth, Kittery and York Street Railway; and the Portsmouth, Dover and York Street Railway. The trackage for this scenic railway totaled ninety miles. Building this railway was the final link to complete the continuous trolley route along the Atlantic coast from New York to Lewiston, Maine.

Initial rolling stock consisted of two twenty-foot closed cars built by the Briggs Carriage of Amesbury, Massachusetts, two eight-bench single open cars, ex-horsecars from the Portland Railroad, two four-wheel baggage trailers, two snowplows and a locomotive. Two of the single open cars were built by Jackson and Sharp of Wilmington, Delaware.

The rail line's carhouse, where the trolleys are stored and repaired, was located near Mill Square in Sandford, and power was provided by a hydroelectric plant on the Mousam River, about midway between Sanford and Springvale.

Articles of association to form the Atlantic Shore Line Railway were filed with the Maine Railroad Commissioners on October 18, 1899. At a hearing at the state house in Augusta on February 7, 1900, opposition to the railway was voiced by some residents of Kennebunkport who didn't want to have an electric railroad traverse their community. These residents asserted that summer residents would leave Kennebunkport if an electric railroad ran through the town because it would bring a large number of

This trolley passenger car can be seen at the Seashore Trolley Museum in Kennebunk. *Author photo.*

tourists that they considered wouldn't be desirable to the summer residents, and all the visiting day tourists would disrupt the tranquility of this coastal village. The railroad commissioners stated their views that while a few summer residents might leave if the railroad was built, more would come, and the general welfare of the people and state must be considered foremost. Accordingly, they approved the charter for the Atlantic Shore Line Railway on February 9, 1900.

In June 1900, the railroad commissioners granted permission to build 1.57 miles of track from Dock Square, Kennebunkport village, to intersect with the Sanford and Cape Porpoise Railway at Town House. This line was completed and opened on July 4, 1900. The merger of the Sanford and Cape Porpoise Railway, the Mousam River Railroad and the Sanford Power Company with the Atlantic Shore Railway was the next step needed, and that was obtained when the Maine legislature authorized this on March 13, 1903. The merger consolidation was completed on April 1, 1904.

A Biddeford route was added on July 24, 1904. Another legislative act took place on February 1, 1906, enabling the Atlantic Shore Line Railway to absorb the Portsmouth, Dover and York Street Railway. Portsmouth and Dover are in New Hampshire. The railroad constructed a fifteen-mile line between Kennebunk and York Beach where it would connect with that line. The connecting lines of these electric railroads were completed, and operation along the route began on July 20, 1907. The goal to link New York City to Lewiston, Maine, was now obtained. The Atlantic Shore Line Railway traveled through quaint villages and along beautiful beaches, rocky shores and jutting peninsulas with views of nearby islands, attracting many tourist excursions.

This railway began as several small railway systems for local needs and not as a tourist train. The first section was built between Springvale and Sanford under the name of the Mousam River Railroad primarily to carry incoming and outgoing freight to the Boston and Maine Railroad. In 1889, this line was extended to Kennebunk, Kennebunkport and Cape Porpoise to access a deep-water freight connection. The Biddeford to Old Orchard line was added in 1904. All these lines were later consolidated with the Portsmouth, Kittery and York Railway. The Atlantic Shore Line Railway was separated into Central, Wester, and Eastern Divisions. The Central Division connected York Beach, Ogunquit, Moody, Webhannet, Wells, the Elms and Kennebunk. The Eastern Division (formerly the Portsmouth, Kittery and York Railway) connected Portsmouth, Dover and Salmon Falls in New Hampshire and Eliot, South Berwick, Kittery, York and York Beach in Maine. The Western Division included the Springvale to Sanford to Cape Porpoise route and carried the most freight.

There are about three miles of bridges and trestles throughout the rail line, the longest trestle being six hundred feet over the channel of the Cape Neddick River.

The Atlantic Shore Line Railway got its power from several sources and included two water-power plants, three steam plants, substations and storage batteries. Feeder power lines were connected at junctions with section insulators and switches. This required extending a ten-thousand-volt transmission system on the Western Division between Dover, New Hampshire, through York to Ogunquit, where it met up with another transmission line from Old Falls. The principal steam plant was at Kittery Point, which served for years as the power supply for the Portsmouth, Kittery and York Railway.

The Boston and Maine Railroad operated rail lines to many of the same points of the Atlantic Shore Line Railway. The competition between these two railroads forced the Atlantic Shore Line Railway to keep prices low to entice passengers to ride its trains rather than those of its competitor. The railway also carried mail. Shipping packages cost about eight cents per mile, and pouched mail cost about three cents a mile. On the Eastern Division, mail was weighed for distances over twenty miles, as on the Boston and Maine. Both the Atlantic Shore Line Railway and the Boston and Maine received forty-two cents per mile per year for this service.

The Atlantic Shore Line Railway is noted for being the first heavy electric freight line in New England.

As mentioned earlier, the present Eastern Division was built in 1892 by manufacturers of Springvale and Sanford to haul freight for its mills to and from the Boston and Maine Railroad. The success of this project led to the Cape Porpoise extension to secure the economics of a deep-water connection. During the summer, the coal used by the mills came by way of Cape Porpoise, where the company had barge-unloading equipment and coal pocket. In the winter, coal cars were also hauled from the Boston and Maine Railroad. About 125 tons a day was the average amount shipped on this division. Lumber and products of the local woolen and other mills constitute most of the remaining freight business. The company was so well satisfied with the financial aspect of this business that it arranged for an independent steamboat line from Boston, called the Eastern Maine Steamship Company, to carry by way of Portsmouth and Cape Porpoise much of the freight now going via the Boston and Maine Railroad. The company's customers preferred the per-mile pricing rather than paying by the tonnage for hauling freight cars. All car charges were therefore made up of a lump sum basis. The three electric locomotives principally used in this work were built by the Laconia Car Company after the railway company's specifications. They weighed forty-five thousand pounds. The company also had three electric locomotives of the boxcar type and had freight cars of standard size and flatcars as well.

By 1908, more and more people preferred to travel by automobile and move freight by trucks, and profits started to diminish rapidly year after year. The company filed for bankruptcy, and new owners purchased the company from the bankruptcy court and incorporated their newly formed company in January 1911, keeping much of the same management team of the previous owners. They attempted to institute economic measures and make improvements to service to attract more business. The improvements were impressive. The old Portsmouth, Kittery and York Railway was rebuilt, eliminating many sharp curves in Kittery and York; trestles were replaced, and new ties and rails were laid throughout the system. Almost every car was taken to the Town House car house for overhauling and painting. Schedules were sped up, too. But the new railway still couldn't make money. The new railway had heavily funded debt, and operating costs were still rising much too fast to compete with the automobile. In 1916, the Atlantic Shore Line Railway entered into an agreement with the Portland Railroad and the Lewiston, Augusta and Waterville Railway to unify freight service all the way from the Androscoggin and Kennebec regions of Maine to the New Hampshire state line. These efforts kept the railroad operating at a marginal profit for several years, but again, it wasn't enough. On March 17, 1923, by order of the Federal Circuit Court at Portland, the Portsmouth, Dover and York Street Railway suspended operations. The railway property was sold off at a foreclosure sale. All twelve miles of track from Kennard's Corner in Eliot to Sea Point in Kittery was torn up and sold for scrap in 1924. Many of the cars were also sold for scrap, and all serviceable rolling stock was moved to the carbarn at Kittery Point. Later that year, the Fitchburg and Leominster Streetway, the Bellows Falls and Saxton's River Railway and the Portsmouth, Kittery and Eliot Railway attempted to take over the Kennard's Corner to Sea Point trackage and revive operations. But they could get little or no support from local businesses, so that attempt failed. In 1925, the railroad was permanently shut down. Everything saleable was disposed and the bondholders were paid off, allowing the discharge of the court-ordered receivership.

As mentioned earlier, ninety towns and cities across Maine had electric railroads. You can find a complete list of all ninety communities in appendix IV.

Light Rail

Light rail evolved from trolleys as a way to transport people and smaller freight loads at higher speeds. Light rail, unlike trolleys, has a dedicated right of way. Light rail has smaller motors, and the cars are less expensive to purchase and operate. Traction motors (DC or AC electric motors) drive the wheels of light rail. The vehicle can be operated by a person or computer. Light rail became more prevalent in the 1930s with the development of "bullet cars." Light rail development is growing today due to overloaded highway systems.

Chapter 13

RAILWAY POST OFFICES

W hen we think of our mail being delivered, we envision walking to the mailbox by our house or going to local post offices to pick it up. The mail is sorted by United States Postal Service (USPS) employees and delivered to local post offices for distribution by truck companies contracted by USPS. Well, it wasn't always that way. In the 1800s, the United States Post Office (USPO) was looking for a better way to get mail sorted and delivered faster. It envisioned sorting the mail along the route rather than the system it had at the time, in which mailbags sat untouched for days waiting to be sorted. This idea proved so successful that an act of Congress on July 7, 1838, declared all railroads postal routes.

By the 1900s, railroads were an essential tool for postal service success. The first railroad cars used by the postal service were wooden and equipped only to sort and distribute letter mail. They later carried first-class mail and packages as well. The mail workers were employees of the railroads and not the U.S. Post Office.

These cars were heated by wood stoves and lighted by oil lamps, so they could be dangerous upon impact from jumping the tracks or a collision. Accidents and unsafe cars were not the only concerns of a railway post office clerk. In the 1920s, train robberies increased as criminals realized mail trains often carried large amounts of money or gold. This was the reason railway post office (RPO) clerks were required to carry .38-caliber pistols.

When exchanging mail, trains slowed down so clerks could transfer mail by hand, which was inefficient and dangerous. This system was later replaced

Railway post office clerks sorting mail in railroad car. Courtesy *Smithsonian Postal Museum*.

by a mail crane, a simple steel hook and crane. Mailbags were hung from the crane and attached at the bottom with the hook. As the train sped by, a mail clerk would raise the train's catcher arm to grab the mailbag. "Mail-on-the-fly" was not easy to master. Clerks had to carefully pay attention and raise the catcher arm from the train at the precise moment. If raised late, the exchange was not made, and the mail was missed during that run. RPO clerks were considered the elite of the postal service's employees.

RPO clerks needed to memorize a lot of things. They worked on multiple routes, so they needed to learn which stations were coming up next on that day's train. If a clerk was a substitute, which was how most started, he had to know countless routes with staggering numbers of towns with post offices that received mail. Clerks finally had to know where connecting trains met so that mail going either north–south or east–west could be delivered to the correct train. The clerk also had to throw that destination's sorted mail from the train. If the bag was not thrown far enough, a "snowstorm" could occur, meaning the mailbag was ripped under the train, scattering the mail.

RPO clerks developed a strong sense of camaraderie. No clerk rested until all work was completed and every piece of mail was sorted. It was a "one for all and all for one" atmosphere in which each took pride in his job and the responsibility of ensuring the mail was delivered. For 140 years, the Railway Post Office carried the mail to be delivered across America.

As highways were built and air travel increased, the U.S. Post Office began to fade out mail trains. By 1965, only 190 trains carried mail; by 1970, no first-class mail was carried on the railroad. The last railway post office, which operated between New York and Washington, D.C., made a final run on June 30, 1977.

All of the major railroads and many of the smaller railroads in Maine sorted and delivered mail. Mail delivery by rail ceased in the late 1960s in Maine.

Chapter 14

THE PORTLAND COMPANY

Locomotive Foundry in Portland

A history of Maine railroads wouldn't be complete without highlighting the impact of the Portland Company. The Portland Company was a locomotive foundry established by John Poor and Septimus Norris to build railroad equipment. The foundry was established in 1846 on Fore Street adjacent to the St. Lawrence and Atlantic, the Portland terminus connection between Portland, Maine, and Montreal, Quebec, Canada.

The Portland Company produced more than 600 steam locomotives from its opening in 1847 until it stopped production in 1978. It also produced 160 merchant and naval vessels, rail cars, construction equipment and Knox automobiles. The Civil War side-wheel gunboats *Agawam* and *Pontoosuc* were also produced here.

The first locomotive, the *Augusta*, was delivered to the Portland, Saco and Portsmouth Railroad, later part of the Boston and Maine Railroad, in July 1848.

Between 1848 and 1853, the Portland Company built twenty-five twenty-two- to twenty-five-ton, 4-4-0 type, five-foot-six-inch-gauge steam locomotives for the St. Lawrence and Atlantic Railroad, which John Poor was instrumental in getting built. It was customary for locomotives to be named. So, here is the list of the twenty-five locomotives built during those years:

1848: two steam locomotives, the *Montreal* and the *Machigonne*
1849: three steam locomotives, the *Oxford*, the *William P. Preble* and the
    Waterville

1850: two steam locomotives, the *Coos* and the *Jenny Lind*

1851: three steam locomotives, the *Felton*, the *Railway King* and the *Casco*

1852: five steam locomotives, the *Forest City*, the *Danville*, the *Consuelo*, the *Falmouth* and the *Daniel Webster*

1853: ten steam engines, the *Cumberland*, the *Norway*, the *Nulhegan*, the *Paris*, the *Gloucester*, the *Yarmouth*, the *Amonoosuc*, the *Vermont*, the *Gorham* and the *J.S. Little*

The Portland Company also started building two-foot-gauge locomotives in 1890 after acquiring the patterns from Hinkley Locomotive Works. The Portland Company modified and improved these patterns, and these designs became the most successful of Maine's two-foot-gauge railroads. Their locomotives had ornate Victorian features including capped domes and a cab roof. The first of these newly designed locomotives was the heaviest and most powerful on the Maine two-foot-gauge railroads at that time. Portland locomotives became the standard for passenger service as larger freight engines were built. Portland locomotives were subsequently used for yard service and on lines with lighter rail. Portland was the

Portland Company complex, Portland, 1938. *Maine Historical Society Item #12551, Collections of Maine Historical Society.*

dominant manufacturer of freight cars for the Maine two-foot-gauge railroads between 1890 and 1907.

The Portland Company attempted to build a larger two-foot gauge based on the original design, but it wasn't successful. After this attempt, the company stopped building two-footers altogether. The original design, however, served Maine two-foot gauge railroads well. The locomotive the company built for the Kennebec Railroad in 1890 remained in service until 1929; the one built for the Wiscasset, Waterville and Farmington Railway in 1894 kept pulling trains until 1933; and the locomotive the Portland Company built for the Monson Railroad in the late 1890s was in operation until 1943.

The Monson Railroad was built for the sole purpose of transporting slate from its own quarry to the Bangor and Aroostook Railroad at Monson Junction for shipment worldwide. The railroad kept hauling slate from this quarry until 1943. The Monson Railroad was known as the "two by six" because the rail line was only six miles long. It connected to the Bangor and Aroostook Railroad at Monson Junction. This railroad also bought six

Monson Railroad locomotive #1, Portland, 1910. *Maine Historical Society Item #12551, Collections of Maine Historical Society.*

flatcars from Laconia Car Company in 1905. The amount of slate from the quarry shipped by this short railroad was significant enough that the Bangor and Aroostook Railroad built a new freight transfer station to handle all the loads from this new shipper.

Fortunately, several locomotives have been preserved. A five-foot-six-inch-gauge locomotive built by the Portland Company can be seen at Canada Science and Technology Museum in Ottawa, Ontario. Several two-foot gauge locomotives have been preserved as well. Two built for the Sandy River and Rangeley Lake Railroad; one built for the Kennebec Railroad; and one built for the Wiscasset, Waterville and Farmington Railway can be seen at the Wiscasset, Waterville and Farmington Railway Museum in Alna, Maine. The engine at the WW&F Museum is the only surviving two-foot engine built by the Portland Company.

Chapter 15

THE FUTURE OF MAINE RAILROADS

T he future of Maine railroads looks promising. Long-distance passenger service returned in 2001. Amtrak's Downeaster makes five round trips daily between Boston and Brunswick with stops along the way in Freeport, Portland, Old Orchard Beach, Saco and Wells, and ridership continues to grow year to year. Further expansion is being studied to continue Amtrak service to Lewiston-Auburn.

Amtrak Downeaster at Amtrak station, Portland. *Author photo.*

Freight is also moving along Maine railroads throughout the entire state over the following railroads:

Pan Am Railways (Amtrak travels on Pan Am Railway tracks)
Eastern Maine Railway (connects to the New Brunswick (Canada) Southern)
Central Maine and Quebec Railway
St. Lawrence and Atlantic Railroad
Turner Island LLC
Maine Northern Railway

There are scenic (tourist) railroads and trolleys operating in Maine as well.

POSTSCRIPT

A s this book went to print, a significant change occurred to the status of Maine's railroads. The Alberta-based Canadian Pacific (CP) Railway purchased the Central Maine and Quebec (CMQ) Railway, elevating Maine's railroads to Class I. Prior to this purchase, Maine had only Class III railroads, which meant the railroads had less than $35,809,698 in total revenue.

By buying Maine's CMQ, the CP will now transport Maine products not only to the Port of Montreal but throughout the entire coast-to-coast network of railroads in Canada. As part of the deal, CP will have ownership of Katahdin Railcar Services, a tank car cleaning and repair facility in Derby, Maine. It will also continue to operate a twelve-mile branch line at the Long Ridge Energy Terminal in Monroe County, Ohio.

This sale will mark the return of a Class I railroad to Maine for the first time since the 1980s. Maine's railroads will now be part of a coast-to-coast rail network run by a company focused on running railroads rather than by an investment firm. Central Maine and Quebec Railway purchased the Montreal, Maine and Atlantic Railway in early 2014, months after a train carrying crude oil went off the tracks in Lac Megantic, Quebec, and exploded into a ball of fire, killing forty-seven people.

One of the most important advantages of having a large railroad operation such as the Canadian Pacific in Maine will be the connectivity. Cargo loaded in Maine will no longer have to be unloaded where the CMQ line ends and transferred to another railroad. This purchase will expand operations not only across the entire length of Canada but also from Kansas City, Missouri, to Maine in the United States. Having Class I railroad service in Maine again will allow more access to not only the ports of Searsport, Maine, and Montreal, Canada, but also to the central United States and the western ports of Canada, thereby opening up opportunities for shipping Maine products to Asia and the Pacific Rim countries.

Canadian Pacific plans to construct a new multimodal transload terminal near Montreal as part of its wider plans to reach eastern markets that are not very rail accessible, including urban areas and those without direct access to rail. This terminal will be located near the Canadian Pacific's Cote Saint-Luc yard in Montreal. Construction is planned in several phases on land CP already owns by June 2020. Phase one, to be completed by June 2020, will be the building of a 118,000-square-foot rail-served facility that will receive, unload, carry and deliver rail traffic while also having opportunities for indoor and outdoor transloading. This facility will be able to support eighteen rail cars inside. More than 4,000 feet of existing and adjacent track will surround the facility. The facility's layout will be constructed to accommodate future expansions. This yard is located near Highways 13, 20, 40 and 250 and close to the Port of Montreal, enabling the railroad to provide customers with trucking and transload services.

This will be a huge boost to the economy of Maine as it again will be serviced by a Class I railroad with total revenues approaching $500 billion—fourteen times more revenue than that of a Class III railroad!

Appendix I

Railroad Museums
and Scenic Rides in Maine

Railroad Museums

Boothbay Railroad Village
586 Wiscasset Road, Boothbay, ME 04437
207.663.4727
railwayvillage.org

Cole Land Transportation Museum
405 Perry Road, Bangor, ME 04401
207.990.3600
www.colemuseum.org/category/exhibits

Maine Narrow Gauge Railroad Company and Museum
58 Fore Street, Portland, ME 04101
207.828.0814
mainenarrowgauge.org

Oakfield Railroad Museum
47 Station Street, Oakfield, ME
207.267.1637
www.facebook.com/Oafieldrailroadmuseum

Seashore Trolley Museum
195 Log Cabin Road, Kennebunkport, ME
207.967.2712
trolleymuseum.org/visit

Wiscasset, Waterville and Farmington Railway Museum
97 Cross Road, Alna, ME
207.882.4193
wwfry.org

Scenic Railroad Rides

Belfast and Moosehead Lake Railroad
13 Oak Hill Road, Belfast, ME 04921
207.772.3899
belfastandmooseheadlakerail.org/portal/index.php

Boothbay Railway Village
586 Wiscasset Road, Boothbay, ME 04537
207.633.4727
railwayvillage.org

Downeast Scenic Railroad
34 High Street, Ellsworth, ME 04605
866.449.7245
www.downeastscenicrail.org

Maine Narrow Gauge Railroad Company and Museum
58 Fore Street, Portland, ME 04101
207.828.0814
mainenarrowgauge.org

Sandy River and Rangeley Lakes Railroad
128 Bridge Street, Phillips, ME 04966
207.639.2228
www.srrl-rr.org

APPENDIX I

Wiscasset, Waterville and Farmington Railway Museum
97 Cross Road, Alna, ME
207.882.4193
wwfry.org

Trolley Rides

Seashore Trolley Museum
195 Log Cabin Road, Kennebunkport, ME 04046
207.967.2800
trolleymuseum.org

RAILROAD STATIONS
STILL IN EXISTENCE IN MAINE

Addison: Built by the Washington County Railroad, privately owned.

Agamenticus: Built by the Boston and Maine Railroad, privately owned.

Albion: Built by the Wiscasset, Waterville and Farmington Railway, home of the Albion Historical Society.

Arundel: Built by the Boston and Maine Railroad, privately owned.

Auburn: Freight depot built by the Maine Central Railroad, used as a business.

Baileyville: See Woodland.

Bath: Built by the Maine Central Railroad. It was rehabilitated by the Bath Transportation Commission and used by the Eastern Maine Railroad for a few years as a tourist train. It ceased operation in 2015, but the station remains.

Belfast: Freight depot built by the Belfast and Moosehead Lake Railroad freight depot.

Benton Station: Built by the Maine Central Railroad, privately owned.

Bethel: Built by the Grand Trunk Railway.

Biddeford: Built by the Boston and Maine Railroad, used as a business.

Bigelow: Built by the Franklin and Megantic Railroad.

Bingham Heights: Built by the Somerset Railroad, privately owned.

Blanchard: Built by the Bangor and Aroostook Railroad, privately owned.

Brooks: Built by the Belfast and Moosehead Railroad.

Brownville Junction: Built by the Canadian Pacific Railroad.

Bryant Pond: Built by the Grand Trunk Railway.

Bucksport: Built by the Maine Central Railroad, home of the Bucksport Historical Society Museum.

Buxton: Built by the Boston and Maine Railroad, privately owned.
Calais: Built by the Washington County Railroad.
Canton: Built by the Maine Central Railroad.
Caribou: Built by the Bangor and Aroostook Railroad.
Cathance: Built by the Maine Central Railroad.
Colombia: Built by the Washington County Railroad, privately owned.
Cornish: Freight Depot built by the Maine Central Railroad.
Cummings: Built by the Boston and Maine Railroad, moved to Johnson Museum in Wells.
Dead River Station: Built by the Maine Central Railroad, used as a business.
Dexter: Former freight depot. Built by the Maine Central Railroad, privately owned.
Dover-Foxcroft: Former freight depot, built by the Maine Central Railroad.
East Hebron: Built by the Maine Central Railroad.
East Sumner: Built by the Maine Central Railroad, privately owned.
East Vassalboro: Built by the Wiscasset, Waterville and Farmington Railway, privately owned.
East Wilton: Built by the Maine Central Railroad, used as a business.
Ellsworth: Built by the Maine Central Railroad.
The Elms: Built by the Boston and Maine Railroad, used as a business.
Enfield: Built by the Maine Central Railroad, moved to Bangor and used as a museum.
Farmington: Built by the Maine Central Railroad, used as a business.
Fort Fairfield: Built by the Bangor and Aroostook Railroad.
Fort Kent: Built by the Bangor and Aroostook Railroad, home of the Fort Kent Historical Society Museum.
Frankfort: Freight depot built by the Bangor and Aroostook Railroad.
Freeport: Built by the Maine Central Railroad, moved to Boothbay Railway Museum.
Frenchville: Built by the Bangor and Aroostook Railroad, used as a museum.
Fryeburg: Built by the Maine Central Railroad, privately owned. Maine Central Railroad's former freight depot here still stands as well, used as a business.
Gardiner: Built by the Maine Central Railroad. Maine Central Railroad's former freight depot still stands here as well.
Georges River: Built by the Maine Central Railroad, used as a museum.
Gilead: Built by the Grand Trunk Railway.
Gorham: Built by the Portland and Rochester Railroad, used as a business.

Great Works: Built by the Boston and Maine Railroad, used as apartments.

Hallowell: Former freight depot. Built by the Maine Central Railroad.

Island Falls: Former freight depot. Built by the Bangor and Aroostook Railroad.

Jackman: Built by the Canadian Pacific Railroad.

Kennebunk: Former freight and passenger depots. Built by the Boston and Maine Railroad, used as businesses.

Kennebunk Beach: Built by the Boston and Maine Railroad, used as a museum.

Kennebunkport: Built by the Boston and Maine Railroad.

Kingfield: Built by the Franklin and Megantic Railroad.

Kittery Point: Built by the York, Harbor and Beach Railroad, privately owned.

Lewiston: Built by the Maine Central Railroad, used as a business.

Lewiston: Original passenger station, built by the Grand Trunk Railway.

Lincoln: Built by the Maine Central Railroad, owned by Pan Am Railways.

Lisbon Falls: Built by the Maine Central Railroad, used as a business.

Machias: Built by the Washington County Railroad.

Madawaska: Built by the Bangor and Aroostook Railroad, owned by the Montreal, Maine and Atlantic Railway.

Marbles Station: Built by the Sandy River and Rangeley Lakes Railroad. The oldest and oldest "stone" railroad station in Maine.

Mechanic Falls: Former freight depot for Grand Trunk Railroad.

Mechanic Falls: Built by the Maine Central Railroad.

Millinocket: Bangor and Aroostook Railroad office building here still stands, owned by the Maine, Montreal and Atlantic Railway.

Milo: Former freight depot, built by the Bangor and Aroostook Railroad.

Monmouth: Former freight depot, built by the Maine Central Railroad.

Monson: Built by the Monson Railroad.

Monson Junction: Built by the Monson Railroad.

New Castle: Both freight depot and passenger station, built by the Maine Central Railroad.

Norridgewock: Built by the Somerset Railroad.

North Anson: Former freight depot, built by the Somerset Railroad.

North Belgrade: Built by the Maine Central Railroad, privately owned.

North Berwick: Built by the Boston and Maine Railroad, used as a business.

Northern Maine Junction: Combination offices/station used by the Maine Central Railroad and the Bangor and Aroostook Railroad.

North Vassalboro: Built by the Wiscasset, Waterville and Farmington Railway, privately owned.

Oakfield: Built by the Bangor and Aroostook Railroad, home of the Oakfield Railroad Museum.

Old Town: Former freight depot, built by Maine Central Railroad, now owned by Pan Am.

Old Town: Passenger station built by the Maine Central Railroad, used as a business.

Orono: Built by the Maine Central Railroad.

Palermo: Built by the Wiscasset, Waterville and Farmington Railway, privately owned.

Parsons: Built by the Boston and Maine Railroad, privately owned.

Patten: Former freight depot, built by the Bangor and Aroostook Railroad.

Phillips: Both freight depot and passenger station, built by the Sandy River and Rangeley Lakes Railroad.

Pittsfield: Built by the Maine Central Railroad.

Poland: Both the freight depot and passenger station, built by the Maine Central Railroad.

Portland: Two former office buildings of the Grand Trunk Railway, used as businesses.

Portland: Offices of the Maine Central Railroad.

Presque Isle: Built by the Bangor and Aroostook Railroad, privately owned.

Princeton: Built by the Maine Central Railroad, used by the local municipal airport for offices.

Richmond: Former freight depot, built by the Maine Central Railroad.

Riverside: Built by the Maine Central Railroad, privately owned.

Rockland: Built by the Maine Central Railroad, used as a business.

Rumford: Both freight depot and passenger station, built by Maine Central Railroad.

Rumford Falls: Built by the Maine Central Railroad, moved to Mechanic Falls.

Saco: Both freight depot and passenger station, built by the Boston and Maine Railroad.

Salem: Built by the Sandy River and Rangeley Lakes Railroad, privately owned.

Sanders Mill: Built by the Sandy River and Rangeley Lakes Railroad, moved to Phillips.

Sanford: Freight depot, built by the Boston and Maine Railroad.

Searsport: Both former freight depot and passenger station, built by the Bangor and Aroostook Railroad, used as a business.

Sherman: Freight depot, built by the Bangor and Aroostook Railroad.

Smyrna Mills: Freight depot, built by the Bangor and Aroostook Railroad.

South Lagrange: Built by the Bangor and Aroostook Railroad, privately owned.

South Paris: Built by the Grand Trunk Railroad.

South Windham: Built by the Maine Central Railroad, used as a business.

Stockholm: Freight depot, built by the Bangor and Aroostook Railroad.

Stockton: Both freight depot and passenger station, built by the Bangor and Aroostook Railroad.

Tapleyville: Built by the Boston and Maine Railroad, moved to Kennebunkport and home of the Seashore Trolley Museum.

Thomaston: Built by the Maine Central Railroad, used as a museum.

Thorndike: Built by the Belfast and Moosehead Lake Railroad, moved to Boothbay Railway Museum.

Troutdale: Built by the Somerset Railroad, privately owned.

Unity: Built by the Belfast and Moosehead Lake Railroad

Vanceboro: Built jointly by the Maine Central Railroad and the Canadian Pacific Railroad.

Waldoboro: Built by the Maine Central Railroad, owned by the Maine Eastern Railroad.

Warren: Built by the Maine Central Railroad.

Weeks Mills: Freight depot, built by the Wiscasset, Waterville and Farmington Railroad.

Wells: Built by the Boston and Maine Railroad, used as a museum.

Wells Beach: Both freight depot and train station, built by the Boston and Maine Railroad.

West Farmington: Built by the Maine Central Railroad, used as a post office.

West Minot: Both freight depot and passenger station, built by the Maine Central Railroad, privately owned.

Whitneyville: Built by the Washington County Railroad.

Wilton: Built by the Maine Central Railroad, used as a business and moved to Jay.

Winslow: Built by the Wiscasset, Waterville and Farmington Railroad, privately owned.

Woodland (Baileyville): Both freight depot and passenger station, built by the Maine Central Railroad.

Yarmouth: The former freight and passenger depots of the Grand Trunk Railroad, both used by businesses.

Appendix III

RAILROADS IN MAINE
THAT BECAME PART OF THE
MAINE CENTRAL RAILROAD COMPANY

Name of Railroad	Charter Year	Years Major Segments Opened	Miles of Line	Location
Androscoggin and Kennebec Railroad	1845	1848–49	55	Danville Jct.– Waterville
Androscoggin Railroad Co.	1848	1852–70	67	Brunswick– Farmington
Bangor & Piscataquis Canal & Railroad Co.		1833–36	12	Bangor–Old Town
Bangor, Milford and Old Town Railroad (later renamed the Veazie Railroad)		1836–69	12	Bangor– Milford
Belfast and Moosehead Lake Railroad		1868–70	33	Burnham Jct.– Belfast
Buckfield Branch Railroad	1847	1850–55	18	Mechanic Falls–E. Sumner

Name of Railroad	Charter Year	Years Major Segments Opened	Miles of Line	Location
Bucksport and Bangor Railroad Co.	1873	1874	19	Bangor–Bucksport
Calais and Baring Railroad Co.	1849	1851–52	4	Calais–Baring
Dexter and Newport Railroad	1888	1889	17	Dexter–Foxcroft
European and North American Railroad	1850	1868–71	114	Bangor–Vanceboro
European and North American Railway	1880	1888–91	4	Enfield–Howland
Kennebec and Portland Railroad Co.	1848	1849–51	71	Portland–Bath–Brunswick–Augusta
Knox and Lincoln Railroad	1864	1871–73	48	Woolwich–Rockland
Lewy's Island Railroad Co.	1854	1856–57	11	Calais–Princeton
Maine Shore Line Railroad Co.	1881	1884	41	Brewer–Hancock Pt. (Mt. Desert Ferry)
Penobscot and Kennebec Railroad Co.	1845	1853–55	55	Waterville–Bangor
Portland and Ogdensburg Railroad Co.	1868	1870–75	91	Portland–Lunenburg, VT
Portland and Oxford Central Railroad Co.	1857	1867–70	7	E. Sumner–Canton
Portland and Rumford Falls Railway Co.	1890	1892–99	38	Rumford–Auburn

Name of Railroad	Charter Year	Years Major Segments Opened	Miles of Line	Location
Rangeley Lakes and Megantic Railroad Co.	1909	1912	8	West Kamenkeag–Kennebago
Rumford Falls and Buckfield Railroad Co.	1874	1879	1	Gilbertville
Rumford Falls and Rangeley Lakes Railroad Co.	1894	1895–1902	40	Rumford–Oquossoc
Sebasticook and Moosehead Railroad Co.	1886	1886–1901	16	Pittsfield–Mainstream
Somerset and Kennebec Railroad Co.	1848	1853–56	37	Augusta–Waterville–Skowhegan
Somerset Railroad Co.	1860	1874–75	25	Oakland–North Anson
Somerset Railway	1883	1888–90	16	North Anson–Bingham
Somerset Railway Co.	1904	1905–7	51	Bingham–Moosehead Lake
Washington County Railroad Co.	1893	1898	115	Ellsworth–Machias–Eastport
Washington County Railway Co.	1903	1906	1	Woodland Jct.–Woodland

Appendix IV

TYPES OF LOCOMOTIVES/RAIL CARS/
TURNTABLES

LOCOMOTIVES

Locomotives are categorized by type using the Whyte system. The first number is the number of guide wheels at the front of the engine, the last number is the number of guide wheels at the back of the engine and the numbers in the middle are the number of driving/powered wheels.

The three major locomotive types are the steam locomotive, the diesel locomotive and the electric locomotive.

Steam Locomotives

A steam locomotive is one that produces pulling power through a steam engine. They are fueled by coal, wood or oil to produce steam in a boiler. The steam moves reciprocating pistons that are connected to the engine's main wheels, also known as driver wheels. Both fuel and water are carried with the locomotive or in wagon tenders pulled behind. Large amounts of water were essential to the operation of these engines. Locomotives had to stop along the route to replenish water. These stops were referred to as "water stops" or "water stations." Fuel had to be replenished, so the train would often load more of the fuel, such as coal or wood, that it used at these stops.

Most of the steam locomotives used in the United States in the 1800s and early 1900s were 4-4-0 type and are also referred to as the "American" type of locomotive.

A 4-4-0 locomotive type is one that has four *leading wheels* on two axles, four powered and coupled *driving wheels* on two axles and a lack of *trailing wheels* on the engine; thus, the classification of 4-4-0.

Leading wheels of a steam locomotive are unpowered wheels located in front of the driving wheels. Leading wheels are used to help the locomotive negotiate curves and to support the front portion of the boiler.

Driving wheels of a steam locomotive are powered wheels that are driven by the locomotive's turbine. The driving wheels are coupled together with side rods, also referred to as coupling rods.

Trailing wheels of a steam locomotive are unpowered wheels located behind the driving wheels. This enabled boilers to be lowered, since the top of the main frames was dropped down behind the driving wheels and under the firebox. The firebox could also be longer and wider, increasing the heating surface area and steam generation capacity of the boiler and, therefore, its power.

Most of the 0-4-4 type steam locomotives used on the two-foot gauge railroads in Maine were made by the Baldwin Locomotive Works or the Portland Company.

Diesel Locomotives

In a diesel locomotive, the prime mover is the diesel engine that is mechanically coupled to the *driving wheels* (drivers). The diesel engine rotates the main generator responsible for producing electricity to power the traction motors that are geared to the drivers.

There are three main types of diesel locomotives; diesel-mechanical, diesel-hydraulic and diesel-electric. The diesel-mechanical and diesel-hydraulic locomotives are best for shorter distances, and the diesel-electric locomotives are best for long-distance hauling because they have higher horsepower and better fuel economy.

Diesel-electric locomotives brought high-speed passenger service to Maine railroads in the late 1930s. After World War II, most railroads started using diesel locomotives, replacing many of the steam engines in use at the time. Diesel-hydraulic locomotives were introduced in the 1950s, but from 1970 on, diesel-electric transmission has dominated.

Electric Locomotives

Electric locomotives are locomotives powered by electricity from overhead lines, a third rail or on-board energy battery or fuel cell storage.

Electric locomotives are very efficient compared with using steam or diesel. They are quieter than steam and diesel locomotives, and there is no engine, exhaust or mechanical noise. They don't have any reciprocating parts, so they are easier on the tracks, reducing maintenance costs. The power plant capacity for electric vehicles is much greater than individual locomotive uses, so they can have a higher output than diesel locomotives and can provide higher short-term surge power to accelerate faster. Electric locomotives are ideal for commuter rail service that requires frequent stops. These locomotives can be used on freight routes with consistently high traffic volume and in areas with advanced rail networks.

There are no electric commuter rail lines operating in Maine presently, and the only trolleys that run today in Maine are the tourist trolleys.

RAILWAY TURNTABLES

A railway turntable or wheelhouse is a device for turning railing rolling stock, usually locomotives, so they can be moved back in the direction they came from. They are most often located near car barns so locomotives and rolling stock can be directed to which bay they want to take them for maintenance. In the case of steam locomotives, railways needed a way to turn the locomotives around for return trips, as their controls were most often not configured to run the locomotives in reverse for extended periods. Moreover, the speed of steam locomotives is much lower when running in reverse.

Diesel locomotives can be operated in either direction, frontward or backward, but they are managed most often as having "front ends" and "rear ends" in reference to the location of the crew cab. When operated as a single unit, the railway companies prefer, and often require, the locomotive to run "front end" first. Sometimes you will see diesel locomotives situated at both ends of a train. When operated this way, the locomotive pointed "front end" first will pull the train in the desired direction.

Turntables are often used to turn observation cars, so their windowed lounge ends face toward the rear of the train.

ELECTRIC RAILROADS
THAT OPERATED IN MAINE

Androscoggin and Kennebec Railway (A&K)
Aroostook Valley Railroad
Atlantic Shore Railway (ASL)
Auburn and Turner Railroad (LA&W)
Auburn, Mechanic Falls and Norway Street Railway
Augusta and Waterville Street Railway
Augusta, Hallowell and Gardiner Street Railway
Augusta, Winthrop and Gardiner Street Railway
Bangor and Northern Railway (BSR)
Bangor, Hampden and Winterport Railway (BSR)
Bangor, Orono and Old Town Railway (BSR)
Bangor Railway and Electric Company (BSR)
Bangor Street Railway (BSR)
Bath Street Railway
Benton and Fairfield Railway
Biddeford and Saco Railroad
Brunswick and Topsham Electric Railroad
Calais Street Railway
Dover and Eliot Street Railway (ASL)
Fairfield and Oakland Street Railway (WF&O)
Fairfield and Shawmut Railway
Kittery and Eliot Street Railway (ASL)
Kittery and York Street Railway (ASL)

Lewiston and Auburn Horse Railroad (LA&W)
Lewiston and Brunswick Electric Railway (A&K)
Lewiston, Augusta and Waterville Railway (A&K)
Lewiston, Brunswick and Bath Street Railway (A&K)
Mousam River Railroad (ASL)
Norway and Paris Street Railway
Penobscot Central Railway
Portland and Brunswick Street Railway (A&K)
Portland and Cape Elizabeth Railway (PRR)
Portland and Yarmouth Electric Railway (PRR)
Portland, Gray and Lewiston Railroad (PLI)
Portland-Lewiston Interurban Railroad (PLI)
Portland Railroad Company (PRR)
Portsmouth, Dover and York Street Railway (ASL)
Portsmouth, Kittery and York Street Railway (ASL)
Rockland, South Thomaston and St. George Railway (RTC)
Rockland, Thomaston and Camden Street Railway (RTC)
Sanford and Cape Porpoise Railway (ASL)
Skowhegan and Norridgewock Railway and Power Company
Somerset Traction Company
Waterville and Fairfield Horse Railroad (WF&O)
Waterville and Fairfield Railway and Light Company (WF&O)
Waterville and Oakland Street Railway (WF&O)
Waterville, Fairfield and Oakland Street Railway (WF&O)
Westbrook, Windham and Naples Railway (PRR)
York Utilities Company (ASL)

MAINE TOWNS THAT HAD ELECTRICAL RAIL SERVICE

The following communities throughout Maine were served by electric railways:

Alfred, Arundel, Auburn, Augusta, Bangor, Bath, Benton, Biddeford, Brewer, Brunswick, Calais, Camden, Cape Elizabeth, Cape Porpoise, Caribou, Charleston, Chelsea, Corinth, Crouseville, Cumberland, East Vassalboro, Eliot, Fairfield, Falmouth, Farmingdale, Freeport, Gardiner, Glenburn, Gorham, Gray, Greene, Hallowell, Hampden, Kenduskeag, Kennebunk, Kennebunkport, Kittery, Lewiston, Lisbon Falls, Litchfield, Lyman, Madison, Manchester, Mechanic Falls, Minot, New Gloucester, New Sweden, North

Vassalboro, Norway, Oakland, Ogunquit, Old Orchard Beach, Old Town, Orono, Owl's Head, Portland, Presque Isle, Rockland, Rockport, Sabattus, Saco, Sanford, Scarborough, Shawmut, Skowhegan, South Berwick, South Monmouth, South Paris, South Portland, South Thomaston, South Windham, Springvale, St. George, Thomaston, Topsham, Turner, Van Buren, Veazie, Wales, Warren, Washburn, Waterville, Webster, Wells, Westbrook, West Gardiner, West Kennebunk, Winslow, Winterport, Winthrop, Woodland, Yarmouth, York and York Beach.

Notes: Calais, Maine, to St. Stephen, New Brunswick, Canada; South Berwick, Maine, to Dover, New Hampshire; Kittery, Maine to Portsmouth, New Hampshire.

Bibliography

Ascher, John. *When the Maine Central Railroad Went to Sea: Train Boats and Boat Trains*. N.p.: M.J.A. Inc., Publisher, 1993.

Brown, William J. *American Colossus: The Grain Elevator, 1843–1943*. N.p.: Colossal Books, 2015.

Cornwall, L. Peter, and Jack W. Farrell. *Ride the Sandy River: Visit the Past on America's Largest Two-Foot Gauge Railroad*. N.p.: Pacific Fast Mail, 1973.

Encyclopedia Americana. "Boston and Maine Railroad." N.p., 1920.

Fishman, Bernard P. *A Story of Maine in 112 Objects*. Thomaston, ME: Tilbury House Publishers, 2018.

Heald, Bruce D., PhD. *Boston & Maine in the 19th Century*. Images of Rail. Charleston, SC: Arcadia Publishing, 2001.

Holt, Jeff. *The Grand Trunk in New England*. 1st ed. Pickering, Ontario, CAN: Railfare Enterprises, 1986.

Jones, Robert C. *Two Feet to Togus: The Kennebec Central Railroad*. N.p.: Evergreen Press, 1999

Karr, Ronald Dale. *Lost Railroads of New England*. 2nd ed. Pepperell, MA: Branch Line Press, 1996.

Kelley, Joel. *The Belfast and Moosehead Lake Railroad*. Unity, ME: North Country Press, 2017.

Lord, Robert F. *Downeast Depots: Maine Railroad Stations in the Steam Era*. N.p.: Robert F. Lord, Publisher, 1986.

MacDonald, Robert L. *Maine Narrow Gauge Railroads*. Charleston, SC: Arcadia Publishing, 2003.

Marcigliano, John. *All Aboard for Union Station*. N.p.: Pilot Press, 1991.
Mead, Edgar T. *Stories from the Two Foot Gauge: Lilliput Trains in Maine, Wales, and Elsewhere*. N.p.: Weedy Rail Publisher, 1993.
Moody, Linwood W. *The Maine Two-Footers: The Story of the Two-Foot Gauge Railroads of Maine*. Berkeley, CA: Howell-North Press, 1959.
Zimmerman, Michael. *The Sunrise Route: A History of the Railroads of Washington County, Maine*. N.p.: CAY-BEL Publishing, 1985.

Links

Abandoned Rails. "The Bangor and Piscataquis Canal and Railroad." www.abandonedrails.com/Bangor_and_Piscataquis_Canal_and_Rail_Road.
Academic. "Maine Central Railroad Company." enacademic.com/dic.nsf/enwiki/11679453.
American-Rails. "Maine Railroads and Railfanning in 'The Pine Tree State.'" www.american-rails.com/me.html.
Amtrak Downeaster. amtrakdowneaster.com.
Arata, Mary E. "Ayer May Weigh Injunctive Relief against Pan Am." *Nashoba Valley Voice*, October 12, 2011. www.nashobavalleyvoice.com/2011/10/12/ayer-may-weigh-injunctive-relief-against-pan-am.
Ashline, Shelby. "Buckland Board of Health: What Can We Do about Dumped Railroad Ties?" *Greenfield Recorder*, July 6, 2017. www.recorder.com/Buckland-Board-of-Health--What-can-we-do-about-dumped-railroad-ties-11134624.
Bangor Public Library. "John R. Graham and the Bangor Railway and Electric Company." digicom.bpl.lib.me.us/bangorhydro_news/62.
Bedford Depot. "About the Billerica & Bedford Railroad." www.bedforddepot.org/history/BBHistory.html.
Belfast & Moosehead Lake Railroad. belfastandmooseheadlakerail.org/portal/index.php.
Boston & Maine Railroad Historical Society. "A Brief History of the Boston and Maine Railroad." www.bmrrhs.org/history-of-the-b-and-m-railroad.
Canfield, Clarke. "State Agrees to Buy Northern Maine Railroad." Boston.com, October 19, 2010. archive.boston.com/news/local/maine/articles/2010/10/19/purchase_okd_for_n_maine_railroad.
Central Pacific Railroad Photographic History Museum. "The Belfast & Moosehead Lake Railroad." www.cprr.org/Museum/BMLRR.

Cook, William. "Railroads in Bangor and Vicinity." Bangor Public Library. digicom.bpl.lib.me.us/railroad_img.

Edaville. "Rides & Attractions." www.edaville.com/thomasland-attractions.

Kingfield, Maine. "History." www.kingfield.me/history.

Narcissus 1912 Renovation Project. "Ninety Communities in Maine Had Electric Railways Service!" narcissus1912.blogspot.com/2016/03/ninety-communities-in-maine-had.html.

Narrow Gauge. "Franklin & Megantic Railroad." www.narrowgauge.iform.com.au/fm.html.

NB Southern. "NBM Railways." www.nbsouthern.com/NBM-railways-railroads.aspx.

Philadelphia Inquirer. "An Investor Believes He's on Track; Banking Heir Timothy D. Mellon Has Poured Millions into Regional Railroads; He's Also Stirred Controversy." www.inquirer.com/archives.

Sandy River & Rangeley Lakes RR. "History." www.srrl-rr.org/museum/history.

Surface Transportation Board. "Frequently Asked Questions." www.stb.gov/stb/faqs.html.

Turners Island. turnersisland.com.

Wiscasset, Waterville & Farmington Railway Museum. wwfry.org.

INDEX

Gorham (locomotive) 117
Graham, John R. 23, 24, 25, 100, 101
Grand Trunk Railway 44, 69, 70, 71, 72, 73, 83, 90, 91
Grand Trunk Railway of Canada 91
Grand Trunk Railway spur 70
Grand Trunk Station 21, 73
Grant, Ulysses S. 22, 40
Great Depression 75, 80, 108
Greyhound Bus Company 88
Guilford Rail System 41, 48
Guilford Transportation/Pan Am Railways 92, 93, 94, 95

H

Hamlin, Hannibal 41
Hercules 86
Hincks, Sir Francis 69
Hinkley & Drury 42
Hinkley Locomotive Works 44, 117
Hitler, Adolf 85
Holland, Charlotte 30
Horn, Lieutenant Werner 85, 86
Howard Clock Company 65
Hurricane Edna 88

I

imperial German spy 84
International Marine Terminal 20, 96, 97
International Paper Company 90
International Railroad Bridge 75
Iron Road Railways 78

Irving, J.D. 49
Irving, K.C. 49
Irving Transportation Services 81
Irving Woodlands 80

J

Jackson & Sharpe Company 58
Jenny Lind 117
Jones, Robert C. 58
J.S. Little 117

K

Katahdin Iron Works Railroad 41, 74
Kennebec Central Railroad 54, 57
Kennebec Railroad 118
Kingfield and Dead River Railroad 53, 54
Knox and Lincoln branch 87
Knox automobiles 116

L

Laconia Car Company 106, 111, 119
land grant college 23
Lee, Robert E. 22, 40
Lewiston and Auburn Electric Light Company 26
Lewiston and Auburn Railroad 70
Lewiston, Augusta and Waterville Railway 25, 100, 104, 112
Lewiston Power Company 20
Libbey, W.S. 25, 26

W

Y

About the Author

Bill Kenny, a former career U.S. Air Force officer and Gulf War veteran, developed an interest in trains from a very young age. From his first train ride at age eleven to his intensive planning and coordination of the movements by rail and ship of military equipment from the United States and Europe for Desert Shield/Desert Storm to the overseeing of railroad operations at Eielson Air Force Base in Alaska and Loring Air Force Base in northern Maine to being involved in a global logistics career that planned and coordinated the movement of large equipment around the world by rail and shipping for major industrial companies, his many railroad experiences have provided a lifelong interest, education and love of railroads and their history.

As an adjunct professor in public and international affairs, international economics and organizational leadership, his experiences obtained from a career involving global economics and shipping by rail enable him to help his many students understand the importance of worldwide economies in today's world through the use of railroads.

The history of Maine railroads is a prime example of how railroads impact economies, and this author, born in Maine and now living near Maine's largest railroad yard, has experienced this firsthand. His realization that Maine's history of railroads needs to be recorded, preserved and appreciated prompted the writing of this, his first book.